THE RAMADAN KITCHEN

To my *Hooyo Macaan*. Where these recipes began.

And to my daughter, *Amaana*, so your Ramadan kitchen will always carry a part of mine. This book is for you.

ILHAN MOHAMED ABDI

THE RAMADAN KITCHEN

NOURISHING RECIPES FROM FAST TO FEAST

PAVILION

INTRODUCTION 6

SUHOOR 16
IFTAR 34
MAINS 68
BREADS 112
SPICES & CHUTNEYS 134
DESSERT 144
DRINKS 164
EID 182

ABOUT THE AUTHOR 216
INDEX 218
ACKNOWLEDGEMENTS 223

Introduction

In the name of Allah, the Most Gracious, the Most Merciful.

The Significance of Ramadan

Ramadan has always been more than a month of fasting. It is a sacred time rooted in spiritual discipline, devotion and mercy. A period when we turn inward just as much as we give outward. It reminds us of our obligations: to pray with intention; to give with sincerity; and to cleanse both heart and habit. Each year, I greet it like an old friend, bringing with it the opportunity to reset not only physically, but also emotionally and spiritually. For me, it has never been solely about abstaining from food and drink. It is about reflection, generosity, prayer and striving – quietly and consistently – to become better.

As the ninth month of the Islamic calendar, Ramadan follows the lunar cycle and arrives slightly earlier each year. Its beginning is marked by the sighting of the new moon, signalling thirty days of fasting from dawn to sunset. In those hours, we abstain not only from food and drink but from distractions, excess and anything that distances us from presence and purpose. The fast is physical, yes, but it is also a deeply spiritual act, a way to draw closer to Allah (God), to renew our intentions, and to quiet the noise of daily life.

There is a stillness that comes with Ramadan, a softening of pace that allows us to notice what is often overlooked. Even in solitude, there is a sense of belonging, knowing that millions around the world are part of the same rhythm, connected through faith.

When the month comes to an end, we mark it with Eid al-Fitr, a celebration that feels both joyful and grounding. It is a day of prayer, of beauty, of abundance. We gather early in the morning for Eid prayer, dressed in our best clothes, before visiting loved ones, sharing meals and exchanging gifts.

As a child, Eid was pure joy. The anticipation the night before, the smell of something sweet in the morning, the thrill of crisp notes from elders tucked into little purses, the excitement of seeing cousins and the comfort of coming home tired and happy. It was happiness, wrapped in every small detail.

Now that I have a child, it feels even more special. I find myself wanting to create that same kind of wonder for her. I tie treats into little bags, wrap presents, slip notes into envelopes and leave them by the door ready for the morning. There is something sacred in preparing joy for others, in passing on what was once given so freely to me. The beauty of the day is not just in what we do, but in how we feel, having come through something meaningful and arriving at its close with hearts that are full.

As the month approaches, I begin to prepare not just my pantry, but my mind. There is a kind of mental, physical and spiritual housekeeping that happens in the weeks leading up to Ramadan. I take stock of what I need to release and what I want to carry with me into the month ahead.

In our home, preparation takes many forms. We ease into an earlier routine, adjusting our sleep and meal times gently. I plan for the practical things like what to cook and what to freeze, but it is the inner shift that matters more. The quiet decision to do things with more care. To speak less. To pray more.

It is not always easy. There are days when energy is low, and the weight of life feels heavy. But in its difficulty, there is mercy. In its quietness, there is so much clarity.

Wherever you are in your journey, whether this is your first Ramadan or one of many, I pray it brings you ease, clarity and closeness. May your fasts be accepted, your prayers answered and your heart feel at peace.

My Story

I was born in Mogadishu, Somalia, but the war began not long after my first birthday. My family fled, seeking safety, which we eventually found in the UK. I have no memories of the city I was born in, just the stories carried by my parents, my aunties and my grandmother, as well as in the food that always found its way back to our table. Dishes like *maraq* (see page 47), *suqaar* (see page 84) and *bariis* (see page 72) were more than just meals. They were vessels of memory, carrying the flavours of a home I never got to grow up in.

Even though I could not remember Mogadishu, my connection to it was never severed. Since 1997, I have been fortunate enough to return to Somalia many times, tracing my roots and building new memories on that soil. I have travelled back as a daughter and now as a mother, taking my own daughter there when she turned one. To watch her touch the red earth, eat fresh mango under the shade of a neem tree and be held by the same hands that once held me made something in me settle. Food, again, was the thread. Whether it was eating freshly caught fish by the coast or rice prepared by family I had not seen in years, every visit nourished a part of me I did not even know was hungry.

Back home in the UK, food remained the heartbeat of our household, especially during Ramadan. As a child, I watched my mother put so much love into every plate, even when she was tired, even when there was so much else to do. *Bur* (see page 132), soup, dates arranged just so. These were not just things we ate; they were rituals that anchored us. There was comfort in the routine, in the clatter of pans, in the familiar smells that drifted through the house at dusk.

Although I was raised deeply within Somali culture, my cooking has also been shaped by my Egyptian heritage. That influence shows up in quiet ways. Sometimes in the spices I reach for, or in the comforting flavours that make their way into my dishes without me even realizing. It was never a loud presence, but always a steady one, folded into our meals over time. Together, these layers of identity made our Ramadan table feel full and familiar, even far from where we started.

Changing Seasons

But as the years passed, so did the seasons of Ramadan. There was a shift that came quietly at first. From being part of a bustling family home to having my own home, where the table was smaller, and the hush of evening felt unfamiliar. Celebrating Ramadan as a newlywed, and now as a mother, brought a different kind of meaning.

It was no longer just about what we cooked, but who we were becoming in the process. There is something tender about the first Ramadan you spend in your own space. You realize how much went into the meals of your childhood – not just the ingredients, but the effort, the rhythm, the intention behind it all. You begin to notice the little things, like how the call to prayer feels different in a quieter house, or how your own hands begin to mirror your mother's when you roll out dough or plate something with care.

My daughter is still far too young to fast, but already I see the seeds being planted. She watches, just like I once did. She notices the change in pace, the shift in atmosphere, the way our home feels softer and more sacred during this time. One day, she will have her own Ramadans, shaped by the memories we are making now. But for the moment, it is enough that she is part of it. Watching; learning; becoming.

And I am realizing now that the baton has been passed. I am the one setting the table, cooking the meals, keeping the rituals alive. There is a quiet pride in that, but also a deep sense of responsibility. I want her to grow up with the same kind of comfort I felt when Ramadan returned, and the knowledge that it will always bring with it a sense of peace, purpose and belonging.

The Beginning of this Book

This is not just a collection of recipes. It is a reflection of movement, of change, of growth. It holds the dishes I grew up with, the ones I learned along the way and the ones I shared during a time when connection felt hard to come by.

In the early days of the Covid lockdown in 2020, I launched what I called my Ramadan Series, a live cooking series where I would prepare meals from scratch, in real time. No polished setups. No behind-the-scenes tricks. Just real food, made in a real kitchen, with people tuning in from their own homes to follow along.

At the time, it felt new, a little chaotic, but also strangely intimate. There was something about being online without the polish, without the 'here's one I made earlier', that made people feel safe to try things for themselves. I wasn't trying to be a chef, I was just a woman in her kitchen, figuring it out, and bringing others along with me. And that resonated.

Over time, that small community grew. What began as a few live viewers turned into thousands watching, cooking, messaging, asking for recipes. I started to realize that this wasn't just a series. It was something people looked forward to. It was helping others find ease in their kitchens, just as I found mine.

That series stayed with me. It reminded me that food does not need to be fancy to be meaningful. That it doesn't have to be expensive to be rich. That there is comfort in a recipe that works, and reassurance in seeing someone else figure it out as they go.

So when I began shaping this collection, I held onto that same spirit. Some of the recipes come from my mother and aunties – dishes that feel like home, no matter where I make them. Others are newer, shaped by life here in the UK and the way I cook now. Together, they tell the story of a kitchen that bridges memory and movement, where tradition and practicality meet.

While many of the recipes in this book are grounded in this, they also reflect the life I've built beyond those borders. They've been shaped by years in the UK, by the people I've shared tables with and by the quiet exchanges that happen online during Ramadan: voice notes from friends; handwritten recipes passed on through generations; ingredients swapped depending on what's available. You'll notice influences from across East and North Africa, from the Middle East and from the wider Muslim diaspora.

They do not belong to just one tradition. Whether inherited, reimagined, or newly formed, every recipe in this book carries a sense of belonging, not to one place alone, but to many.

These are meals for real life. Some can be made ahead. Some can be frozen. Some are for the quiet nights when your energy is low, and others for when the house is full and there is joy in the air. They are not about perfection. They are about showing up, with what you have, with where you are, with love at the centre of it all.

And while many of these dishes are often made during Ramadan and Eid, they are not limited to those occasions. They are meals that can live in your kitchen year-round. Familiar enough to return to often, and flexible enough to suit whatever season you are in.

Planning with Intention

If there is one thing that I have learned over the years, it is that a bit of planning before Ramadan makes a big difference. On the days when time is short or energy is low, having a few things in place can take the pressure off. Whether you are observing Ramadan or just trying to stay organized during a busy season, the last thing anyone wants is to feel rushed or flustered in the kitchen.

It helps to take stock of what the staples are for your own family: the ingredients you reach for often; the meals everyone looks forward to so you can plan in a way that feels manageable rather than overwhelming. Mapping out the bulk ingredients you rely on most, like lentils, rice, flour, or the spices that form the backbone of those meals, can make all the difference. A little preparation goes a long way in keeping the days smoother, not just during Ramadan, but throughout the rest of the year too.

I buy meat in bulk and portion it into freezer bags – cubes for stews, mince for *sambuus* (see page 48), chicken for grilling. I batch-make *sambuus*, freezing them flat so I can take out only what we need each day. I chop onions, garlic and coriander, pack them into ice cube trays with a drizzle of oil, then tip them into freezer bags. It is the kind of quiet prep that makes everything smoother later.

If I have the time, I cook down tomato bases, stews, and a few hearty sauces in advance. I always try to make a couple of chutneys or dipping sauces before the first fast begins. Stored in jars, they last the month and bring something bright to every table.

There is something almost symbolic about sorting through the spice cupboard before Ramadan begins, clearing out what is old, organizing what remains. It may not feel like a small task, and often it is not, but it creates a sense of clarity. A quiet gesture that makes space for what is to come.

Some years, I go all in. I stock the freezer, label every bag, make sauces, and plan out meals. Other years, I do very little. Life takes over, or the energy simply is not there. I have come to understand that Ramadan does not have to look the same every time. Each year arrives at its own pace, and not all of them allow for the same kind of preparation and that is okay. Still, I have found that even small steps in the kitchen can shift the mood of the whole month. A bit of order where you can manage it often brings a sense of ease, and that ease spills over into everything else.

It also helps stretch what we have. Buying in bulk and using what is already in the cupboards can ease the financial strain many of us feel during this time. Less waste. Fewer last-minute trips to the shop.

Over the years, I've learned that where I shop makes a difference too. For many of the recipes in this book, your local greengrocer or butcher will likely have exactly what you need. The coriander is fresher. The garlic comes in larger nets. The meat is often better quality, sold in bigger portions and at a lower price than the supermarket. I also buy large bags of spices I know I'll reach for again and again: cumin, coriander, turmeric, cinnamon, and paprika for example.

It's the same with the pantry. I pick up cans of *fuul* and chickpeas, jars of tomato paste, and anything else I know we'll use over the month. I'm not stockpiling, just planning gently. Shopping this way allows me to feel more prepared without feeling overwhelmed.

And for many of us, the kitchen is not only for those who are fasting. It is also for the toddlers asking for snacks, the elders who still need lunch, or the family members who are not observing. Planning ahead helps us find that middle ground too. The in-between space where everyone is cared for.

Ramadan shifts with us. Some years feel full and abundant. Others feel quiet and stripped back. But whatever kind of Ramadan you find yourself in this year, know that it is enough. That you are enough. Whether you are preparing every detail or just taking it one day at a time, you are showing up. And that matters.

It also helps to know where to look. These small trips to familiar shops – greengrocers, butchers, corner stores – become part of the rhythm too. And over time, they feel like another form of care.

This book is filled with that same kind of care. It was written with my daughter in mind, and for the one day she might turn to these pages the way I turned to the quiet instructions of my own mother. I hope this book feels timeless – not because trends don't change, but because care doesn't. May it be something she returns to, whether she's cooking her first iftar or preparing to host her own family one day, God willing.

And if you are reading this far from your family or your roots, I hope this book brings a sense of connection. I hope it reminds you of something familiar, even if it is not exact. That it helps fill the space between where you are and where you came from. That it makes the kitchen feel a little warmer. That it offers a thread back.

A Note Before You Begin

I hope these pages feel like a conversation between us. A quiet nudge to make something from scratch. To pass something down. To reconnect. I hope they remind you, as they remind me, that even when we are far from where we started, we still carry the warmth of those kitchens with us.

You might find yourself here at the beginning of your journey, or perhaps many Ramadans in. Maybe you are cooking for one, or for a family. Maybe you are holding onto old traditions or building new ones from the ground up. And perhaps you are not observing Ramadan yourself but are here out of curiosity or the simple love of good food. Whichever way you come to this book, know that there is room for you in it.

Some recipes will feel familiar. Others might be new. Some you'll follow exactly. Others you'll adapt without even thinking. This isn't a manual. It's not a checklist. It's a place to land. To try. To taste. To remember. And to begin again, each day, with a little more ease and a little more intention.

And if you find yourself reading this during a season of change, whether it's your first Ramadan away from family, or your first time preparing the meal instead of simply showing up to it, I hope this book meets you there. I hope it keeps you company in the kitchen, gently guiding you through each day. I hope it gives you something to return to, even outside of Ramadan, whenever you need the comfort of something simple, grounding, and good.

This is not just my Ramadan kitchen. It is yours too. I hope it serves you well.

Welcome to *The Ramadan Kitchen*.

SUHOOR

Suhoor is the pre-fasting meal eaten just before sunrise. It's a quiet but meaningful moment that marks the start of each day during Ramadan. Though only a short period of time, and often made while still half-asleep, this meal holds so much intention. It helps nourish the body ahead of a long fast, but just as importantly, it offers a moment of calm and connection before the day begins.

When I think back to my childhood, I remember waking up for suhoor not because I had to, but because the house was already stirring. I'd hear pots gently clinking, voices in low tones, the soft glow of the kitchen light breaking into the darkness. I'd shuffle into the room still wrapped in sleep, too young to fast but curious to be part of it all. There was something about those early hours that felt sacred, even then, before I fully understood why.

As I grew older and began fasting myself, suhoor took on new meaning. It became my first act of participation in Ramadan, something that felt like a quiet step into adulthood. I'd wake up groggy but determined, often sitting in silence as I ate whatever was prepared, learning that this meal wasn't about fullness, but about intention. Over time, it became less of a challenge and more of a ritual – something grounding, something I looked forward to.

Now, I wake up for suhoor with my husband. Our mornings are sometimes still and quiet, sometimes filled with conversation, sometimes just the clatter of plates and the boiling of water for tea. It's a part of Ramadan I've grown to cherish. Even on the hardest mornings, when sleep pulls heavily and the idea of food is uninviting, we still make the effort. And somehow, those are the mornings I remember the most – when it would have been easier to stay in bed, but we chose to rise together.

Suhoor doesn't have to be complicated. Some days, it's toast with peanut butter, or a bowl of oats, or dates with a cup of tea. Other days, I take the time to make something a little more delicate – like *Umm Ali* (see page 30), a sweet, aromatic bread pudding that's warm, comforting and just indulgent enough to feel like a quiet treat before the fast begins. There's comfort in both: the ease of the simple meals, and the joy that comes from preparing something special, even if it's just for yourself.

The recipes in this chapter are a reflection of those rhythms. Some are dishes I've been making since I was young, others are more recent favourites. All of them have brought me comfort in the early hours of Ramadan – each one part of my story. Whether you're cooking for yourself or for loved ones, I hope these dishes offer both ease and delight, and remind you that even the quietest moments can be full of meaning.

SERVES 2

This is yet another celebration of my love for dates – simple, naturally sweet and packed with fibre. It's a great way to use up all the excess dates during Ramadan. For an extra creamy texture, try blending in a banana or substituting the milk with yogurt.

Date Shake

4–5 large Medjool dates, pitted
400 ml/1¾ cups preferred milk
pinch of ground cinnamon
pinch of salt
vanilla extract or sweetener (such as honey, sugar or syrup), to taste (optional)

Place the pitted dates, milk, cinnamon and salt into a blender. Blend until smooth and creamy. (If the dates are firm, you can soak them in hot water beforehand to make blending easier.)

Optionally, add sweetener or vanilla extract to taste.

SERVES 4

Lahsa is Yemen's take on baked eggs in spiced tomato sauce, and it immediately reminded me of the Somali-style shakshuka I grew up with – a comforting, saucy staple in so many homes. But when I first tried it with melted cheese on top, everything changed. It lifts the dish in the most unexpected way, adding richness without overpowering the flavours, and now I can't imagine making *lahsa* without it. With eggs and cheese, it's a naturally protein-rich option that works especially well for suhoor.

Yemeni Lahsa *Stewed Spiced Tomatoes with Eggs and Soft Cheese*

60 ml/¼ cup olive oil
1 onion, finely chopped
2 large tomatoes, finely chopped
1 green chilli (chile), chopped, seeds left in
1 tsp salt
1 tsp black pepper
1 tsp ground cumin
1 tsp ground coriander
1 tsp sweet paprika
1 tbsp tomato purée (paste)
4 eggs
2–3 tbsp soft cheese (I use Puck cheese)
chopped fresh coriander (cilantro), to garnish

Heat the olive oil in a frying pan (skillet) over medium heat. Once hot, add the onion and cook, stirring occasionally, until softened and slightly browned.

Add the tomatoes and chilli, stirring to combine, and cook for 1–2 minutes. Stir in the salt, pepper, cumin, coriander, paprika and tomato purée, mixing well. Allow the mixture to cook down for 3–4 minutes until the oil begins to separate and the tomatoes have fully broken down.

Crack the eggs directly into the pan and immediately mix them into the sauce. Pour in the 60 ml/¼ cup of water and stir until well combined. Dollop and spread the cheese evenly over the top, cover the pan, and let it cook for 2–3 minutes until the eggs are just set.

Garnish with freshly chopped coriander and serve hot.

SERVES 1

Rolex is a well-loved street food that first became popular in Uganda and has since become popular across parts of East Africa. Despite the name, it has nothing to do with watches; 'rolex' is a playful shortening of 'rolled eggs', which is exactly what it is. This version of rolex uses *kimis* instead of chapati, and fills it with an omelette – and it works perfectly.

Rolex *Rolled Omelette with Flatbread*

1–2 eggs
1 tomato, finely chopped
¼ red onion, finely chopped
1 tbsp chopped coriander (cilantro)
pinch of Vegeta or all-purpose seasoning
2 tbsp olive oil
1 kimis (see page 123)

Crack the egg(s) into a bowl, add the tomato, red onion, coriander and a pinch of Vegeta and whisk until well combined.

Heat the oil in a frying pan (skillet) over medium heat. Once hot, pour in the egg mixture, spreading it evenly across the pan. Cook until the underside is set, then carefully flip it over.

Immediately place the kimis on top of the egg and let it cook briefly to allow the egg to adhere to the flatbread.

Remove from the pan, flip onto a plate, and roll it up tightly while still warm. Cut in half or quarters and serve.

Tip: For added flavour, spread your favourite toppings or sauces on the flatbread before rolling.

SERVES 4

Umm Ali is one of my favourite dishes from my mum, and a comforting reminder of her Egyptian heritage. The name translates to 'Mother of Ali', and the dish, often called Egypt's national dessert, is a rich, sweet pudding that resembles a Middle Eastern take on bread pudding. I make mine with croissants, and you can use stale ones if you have any (I never seem to), as they soak up the milk and cream beautifully. You can play around with the toppings: a handful of sultanas (golden raisins), your favourite nuts or both. It's indulgent, surprisingly easy to make and the kind of dessert that always feels special whether it's for suhoor, after iftar, or part of your Eid spread.

Umm Ali *Croissant Bread Pudding*

3 large croissants
1 tbsp granulated sugar
2 tbsp desiccated (dried unsweetened shredded) coconut
2 tbsp toasted flaked (sliced) almonds
2 tbsp crushed pistachios, plus extra to serve
350 ml/1½ cups milk (any milk will work)
400 ml/1¾ cups double (heavy) cream
140 ml/½ cup plus 1 tbsp condensed milk, plus extra to serve
1 large cinnamon stick
4 cardamom pods, cracked open

Preheat the oven to 180°C fan/200°C/400°F/gas mark 6.

Tear the croissants into small pieces and place them in a bowl. Add the sugar, 1 tablespoon of the desiccated coconut, 1 tablespoon of flaked almonds and 1 tablespoon of crushed pistachios. Mix well to coat the croissants. Transfer the mixture to a baking dish and bake for 6–8 minutes until slightly toasted.

Meanwhile, in a saucepan, combine the milk with 250 ml/1 cup of the double cream, 125 ml/½ cup of the condensed milk, the cinnamon and cardamom. Cook over low heat for 8–10 minutes, stirring occasionally.

Remove the dish from the oven and pour the milk mixture evenly over the croissants. In a separate bowl, whisk the remaining cream until thick. Spoon the whipped cream over the croissant mixture. Top with the remaining coconut, almonds and pistachios, then drizzle with the remaining condensed milk.

Return the dish to the oven and bake for 20 minutes.

If you like, drizzle another tablespoon of condensed milk over the top and sprinkle with extra pistachios before serving hot.

SERVES 4

I grew up and still live in Britain, where baked beans are practically a national staple, but the canned kind, which never really made it onto our table except to dress a jacket potato. Instead, we had *fasooliyad* – Somali-style beans – simmered slowly with onions, garlic and spices until thick and full of flavour. I like to call it 'posh beans' – a little richer, a lot more satisfying and packed with goodness. I recently started to use a five-bean mix for added nutrition and texture, but any combination works.

Fasooliyad *Spiced Beans*

2 tbsp olive oil
1 small red or white onion, finely chopped
1 red (bell) pepper, sliced
1 green finger chilli (chile), finely chopped, seeds left in
415-g/14-oz can five mixed beans or regular baked beans
1 tsp ground coriander
1 tsp vegetable or chicken bouillon
1 tsp salt
fresh coriander (cilantro), to garnish
shredded spring onion (scallion), to garnish
bread, to serve

Begin by heating the oil in a frying pan (skillet) over medium heat. Add the onion and cook until softened; about 5 minutes.

Stir in the red pepper and green chilli, mixing well, and allow them to fry for another 3–5 minutes until soft.

Pour in the beans with a splash of water, stirring until well combined. Add the ground coriander, bouillon and salt, then mix everything together. Using the back of a wooden spoon, gently press down on the beans, crushing about half to thicken the sauce. Cover the pan and let it simmer on low heat for 5 minutes.

When ready, garnish generously with fresh coriander and spring onions and serve warm with bread.

SERVES 4

I used to work with someone who made these every single week. She'd bring them into work and heat them up for breakfast, and I remember thinking how clever that was. These became a regular feature in our kitchen when my toddler was weaning, and soon they became a suhoor staple for the family. You can skip the chopping and throw everything straight into a blender, eggs included, if you like. They're easy to prepare in batches and you can customize them with whatever you have on hand: leftover vegetables, cheese, herbs, anything goes. They freeze well too, perfect for those mornings when you don't feel like cooking.

Egg Bites

2 tbsp olive oil
1 red onion, finely chopped
6–8 mushrooms, finely chopped
1 red (bell) pepper, finely chopped
5 eggs
25 g/1 oz/½ cup spinach, chopped
¼ tsp salt
¼ tsp black pepper
45 g/1½ oz/½ cup grated cheese (such as Cheddar or mozzarella) or 60 g/2 oz/½ cup crumbled feta

Equipment
6-hole muffin pan, lightly oiled

Preheat the oven to 175°C fan/195°C/400°F/gas mark 6.

Heat a frying pan (skillet) over medium heat and add 1 tablespoon of oil. Once hot, add the onion, mushrooms and pepper. Cook for 6–8 minutes until softened, stirring occasionally.

While the vegetables cook, crack the eggs into a bowl with a spout. Add the chopped spinach, salt and black pepper, and whisk until well combined.

Divide the sautéed vegetables equally among the holes of the muffin pan, then carefully pour in the egg mixture, leaving some space at the top as they will rise during baking. Top each cup with a sprinkle of cheese.

Place the muffin pan in the oven and bake for 30 minutes, or until the eggs are fully set. Allow the muffins to cool slightly before running a butter knife around the edges to loosen them.

These can be served immediately or stored in the refrigerator for up to 3 days. They can also be frozen for up to 3 months. To reheat, microwave for 30 seconds if thawed, or for 1–2 minutes from frozen.

SERVES 4

Sareen is as simple as it gets. Put simply, it is a barley porridge, but don't let that fool you. It's surprisingly filling, comforting and the kind of dish that sticks with you, especially during Ramadan. Across the Horn of Africa and the Middle East, you'll find similar dishes, such as *talbina* in the Arab world, made with barley flour and praised in prophetic tradition for its soothing, healing qualities. *Sareen* is a humble meal that has quietly nourished generations across the Islamic world. It's best eaten fresh, with ghee and a little sugar on top, although you can easily adapt this to accommodate your favourite toppings, and it will keep you going throughout the day.

Sareen *Barley Porridge*

150 g/5 oz/¾ cup pearl barley
3 tbsp basmati rice
¼ tsp salt
Greek yogurt, milk or ghee, to serve
sugar or honey, to serve

Wash the pearl barley and rice thoroughly and rinse until the water runs clear.

In a large pot, bring 2.5 litres/10½ cups of water to the boil over high heat. Once boiling, carefully add the barley and rice to the pot with the salt, reduce the heat to medium, and stir. Leave to cook for 1½ hours, stirring every 20–30 minutes to ensure it doesn't stick to the bottom of the pot.

When the barley and rice are tender, remove the pot from the heat.

Serve warm with ghee, Greek yogurt or milk with sugar or honey.

If freezing, allow the porridge to cool before transferring it into individual lidded containers. Store in the freezer for up to 1 month.

When ready to serve, defrost the porridge in the fridge. Reheat gently on the stove, adding a splash of water or milk if needed to achieve your desired consistency.

MAKES 4

This is a nostalgic dish that's usually made for children, though it's just as loved by adults. It's made by sandwiching lightly sweetened eggs between two *laxoox*, which is then cooked until golden. It's a great way to use up leftover *laxoox* and makes for a lovely sharing dish. When time and energy are low, it's an easy option to get on the table and perfect for sharing in those quiet early hours.

Laxoox (Canjeero) with Sweetened Eggs
Fermented Pancakes with Sweetened Eggs

8 laxoox (see page 117)
4 eggs
4 tsp granulated sugar or honey
8 tsp sunflower oil

Heat a non-stick frying pan (skillet) over medium heat. Once the pan is warm, place 1 laxoox in the pan with the brown side facing down.

In a small bowl, whisk 1 egg until smooth, then spread it evenly over the top of the laxoox. If using sugar, sprinkle 1 teaspoon of sugar over the egg layer. Place a second laxoox on top, sandwiching the egg.

Pour 1 teaspoon of oil directly into the pan around the edges of the laxoox to help crisp the bottom. Cook for 2 minutes, allowing the egg to set and the base to become slightly crispy.

Drizzle another teaspoon of oil over the top of the laxoox stack, and carefully flip it using a spatula. Cook the second side for 1 minute, or until golden brown.

Remove the stack from the pan and transfer it to a plate. If using honey, drizzle 1 teaspoon of honey over the top. Use a sharp knife or kitchen scissors to divide the stack into four portions and serve immediately. Repeat with the remaining laxoox and eggs.

There is nothing quite like that first bite after a long day of fasting. It's quiet, intentional and deeply comforting. The stillness just before sunset gives way to movement – the table being laid, the clinking of glasses, the pause as everyone waits for the call to prayer. Then, with a date in hand and water on the tongue, the fast is broken. That moment never loses its meaning, no matter how many times you experience it.

Iftar doesn't begin with a feast. It begins with small, simple things. Bites that are just enough to bring your energy back without overwhelming the senses. It's a soft landing after a long day of stillness and patience. These early dishes fill the space between the fast and the evening meal. You eat slowly, just enough to feel steady again, then pause, pray and return to the table later for more.

Growing up, these moments were filled with noise and movement. Family drifting in and out of the kitchen, checking on pots, adjusting platters, calling out how many minutes were left. Now, I share those evenings with my husband. We move around each other in the kitchen, both tired, both hungry, but quietly excited for what we're about to eat. It's never about how much food there is, or how perfectly it's plated. It's the feeling of arriving, together, at this peaceful moment. There's a kind of intimacy to it, setting the table, warming the food, quietly counting down the minutes together. It's one of the parts of Ramadan I love most.

Some of these small bites appear only during Ramadan, and maybe that's why they feel so special. *Bur kuus kuus* (see page 38) – golden, syrup-drenched mini doughnuts – are made for this time of year. As a child, I remember how quickly they would vanish from the table, still warm from the pan. Not much has changed there, they barely make it off the tray before they're gone. *Sambuus* (see page 48), crisp and generously filled, are another favourite. They mark the season, and while they can be made throughout the year, there's something about eating them during Ramadan that makes them feel like a celebration. And yes, Somali *sambuus* really are something special. Some of these dishes stay on the table and are eaten again with the mains later on. They're not confined to a course, they float between moments, picked at slowly, shared and enjoyed in between conversation and prayer.

This chapter brings together the recipes I return to year after year. The ones I prepare first as the sun sets and the fast comes to an end. However you serve them, these dishes serve to ease you into the evening, to savour the moment, and to make the most of that beautiful pause between hunger and fullness.

SERVES 4–6

Also known as *quraac*, *bur kuus kuus* are balls of sweet, puffed fried dough. The name translates simply: 'bur' means 'flour' and 'kuus' means 'something small'. They are ever so slightly crisp on the outside, soft inside and always one of the first things to disappear from the Ramadan table.

You'll find very similar versions in other cultures: *puff puff* in West Africa; *luqaimat* in the Middle East. The toppings can include honey and condensed milk, but nothing tops a proper syrup soak – just make sure the syrup is hot when drizzling if the dough balls have cooled.

Some people are particular about shaping their *bur kuus kuus* into perfect circles, but as a home cook, I find joy in them not being perfect. They hardly ever make an appearance outside of Ramadan, which makes them feel even more special.

Bur Kuus Kuus *Syrup-Soaked Fried Dough Balls*

350 g/12 oz/2½ cups plain (all-purpose) flour
½ tsp salt
2–3 tbsp granulated sugar
1 tbsp fast-action dried yeast
¾ tsp ground cinnamon
300 ml/1¼ cups milk, warmed
sunflower oil, for frying

For the syrup
100 g/3½ oz/½ cup granulated sugar

In a large mixing bowl, combine the flour, salt, sugar, yeast and cinnamon. Slowly pour in the warm milk while stirring, mixing until a smooth, thick batter forms. Once well combined, use your hands to gently beat the batter, incorporating air to create a light texture. Cover the bowl with a clean cloth and let the dough rise in a warm place for about 1 hour, or until it has doubled in size.

While the dough is rising, prepare the sugar syrup. In a small saucepan, combine the sugar with 125 ml/½ cup of water. Bring the mixture to a boil over medium heat, stirring occasionally until the sugar dissolves and the syrup thickens slightly. Remove from the heat and set aside to cool.

Once the dough has risen, use a spoon to gently deflate it and remove any air bubbles.

Continues overleaf

Heat oil in a deep pan over medium-high heat until it reaches 180°C/350°F, or until a cube of bread browns in 30 seconds. Keep a small bowl of water nearby to dip your hands in, which will help prevent the dough from sticking. With wet hands, pinch off small portions of dough, about a tablespoon each, and carefully drop them into the hot oil. Work quickly for even cooking and fry in batches being careful not to overcrowd the pan. Alternatively, you can use one spoon to scoop the dough and another to gently scrape it into the oil.

Fry the dough for 3–4 minutes, or until golden brown on all sides. The dough balls should naturally turn over in the oil, but if they don't, use a slotted spoon or a fork to gently flip them. Once golden, remove them from the oil and drain on a wire rack or paper towels to remove excess oil.

When ready to serve, drizzle the sugar syrup over the dough balls.

SERVES 6–8

This recipe comes from my maternal aunt, one of the most nutritionally wise people I know, always making food that feels good and tastes even better. I'll be honest, I've never been big on raisins (aside from the recent exception of adding them to rice), but she completely changed my mind with this dish. The sweetness of the fruit against the crunch of raw vegetables just works in a way that I didn't expect. And if the raw broccoli worries you, don't let it. The vinegar softens it perfectly. It's vibrant, fresh and surprisingly addictive. I love it most with rice, but it holds its own next to any meat or fish dish.

Broccoli Slaw

360 g/12 oz broccoli
½ large brown onion, finely chopped
1 pink lady apple, chopped
70 g/2½ oz/½ cup sunflower seeds
70 g/2½ oz/½ cup raisins

For the dressing
3 tbsp mayonnaise
3 tbsp Greek yogurt
juice of 1 lemon
1 tbsp apple cider vinegar
1 tsp English mustard
½ tsp black pepper
⅓ tsp salt

In a bowl, whisk together the dressing ingredients until fully combined and smooth. Set aside.

Next, shred the broccoli. To do this, you can use one of the following methods: very finely chop it with a sharp knife; break it into florets and then pulse in a blender; or use a cheese grater. I prefer grating the broccoli directly into a large mixing bowl. Once shredded, add the onion, apple, sunflower seeds and raisins to the bowl. Stir gently to combine.

Spoon the dressing over the salad and use two large spoons to toss and coat everything evenly. Take your time to ensure the dressing is well distributed. Cover the bowl and refrigerate for at least 1 hour. This allows the broccoli and onions to soften.

SERVES 6–8

Everyone has that one food that feels essential during Ramadan. The thing that, if it's missing from the table, makes the evening feel incomplete. For me, it's *bajiye*. They are crispy, golden and usually served with a side of *bisbaas*. They're often described as falafel, but they're not. The method is similar, but the flavour is entirely different. Traditionally, they're made with black-eyed beans (black-eyed peas), but I find the process is rather long, and this version is just as good. The name comes from the Hindi word 'bhaji', a sign of the Indian influence on this dish. You'll often find them sold as street food or during afternoon tea, still warm from the oil, and impossible to resist.

Bajiye *Split Pea Fritters*

300 g/10½ oz/1½ cups yellow split peas
6 garlic cloves
1 small onion
3 green chillies (chiles)
1 tbsp ground cumin
1 tsp salt
2 tbsp self-raising (self-rising) flour
sunflower oil, for frying
Bisbaas Cagaar (see page 141), to serve

Start by washing and rinsing the lentils thoroughly, then place them in a bowl and cover with water, ensuring they are fully submerged. Cover the bowl and leave the lentils to soak for at least 12 hours, or up to 24 hours for softer results.

When ready to use, drain the lentils and transfer them to a blender. Add the garlic, onion and chillies. Blend until combined, scraping down the sides of the blender as needed. Gradually add 60–125 ml/¼–½ cup water; the amount of water needed depends on the softness of the lentils and the strength of the blender. Aim for a smooth but slightly thick batter-like consistency. If blending is difficult, work in batches.

Transfer the blended mixture to a large mixing bowl. Stir in the cumin, salt and self-raising flour until fully incorporated.

Heat the oil in a small pan over medium heat until it reaches 180°C/350°F, or until a cube of bread browns in 30 seconds. Once the oil is hot, use one tablespoon to scoop up a portion of the mixture, and use a second spoon to gently drop the batter into the oil. Repeat, ensuring not to overcrowd the pan. Cook each batch for 3–4 minutes, turning halfway through cooking, until golden brown on both sides.

Remove using a slotted spoon and place on a plate lined with paper towels to absorb any excess oil. Serve with bisbaas cagaar.

SERVES 4-6

Maraq simply means 'soup', but for Somalis, it's so much more than that. You know how people say 'chicken soup for the soul'? Somali *maraq* is exactly that. It's what's brought to the table when someone is unwell, when guests arrive or just to round off a meal. It doesn't matter the occasion – *maraq* always fits. I grew up seeing it served in all kinds of moments, from quiet evenings to celebratory meals. We use goat meat, as that is what is most readily available in Somalia, but lamb is a perfect substitute. Although overall it's very simple, the broth is deeply nourishing with a contrast in textures from the tender, falling-off-the-bone meat to the soft cabbage. It's the kind of dish that feels restorative and grounding, perfect for Ramadan.

Maraq *Lamb and Vegetable Broth*

1 kg/2 lb 4 oz lamb shoulder on the bone, meat diced
small handful fresh coriander (cilantro)
½ onion, quartered
1 tomato, halved
2 potatoes, peeled and quartered
2 carrots, peeled and halved
½ white cabbage, stalk removed and halved
2 green finger chillies (chiles), tops removed, seeds left in
2.5-cm/1-inch piece of ginger, peeled and finely chopped
3–4 garlic cloves, crushed
1 tsp ground cumin
1 tsp ground coriander
2 tsp vegetable bouillon powder
salt, to taste
lemon wedges, to serve
Bisbaas cagaar, to serve

Add the lamb, fresh coriander and 2 litres/8 cups of water to a large saucepan. Bring to a gentle simmer and cook for 40 minutes to develop a flavourful stock. Once done, you can remove the coriander, if preferred.

Add the remaining ingredients to the stock and stir well to combine, ensuring everything is submerged. If the liquid level seems low, add more water as needed, and adjust the salt accordingly. Cover with a lid and simmer for another 30 minutes, or until the potatoes are tender but still hold their shape.

Serve hot with lemon wedges for squeezing over and bisbaas cagaar.

MAKES 12–15

When it comes to *sambuus*, the filling is everything. Beef is by far the most popular. It shows up across countless cultures, and for good reason. These ones are intentionally not packed with vegetables. I've always felt a *sambuus* should be mostly meat. If you want something slightly different, I recently added a little dill to the beef filling, which isn't traditional but honestly works so well. It adds a subtle freshness that caught me off guard in the best way.

Tuna *sambuus* are especially common in southern Somalia and have become my favourite over time, thanks to my aunt, who's like a second mum to me. Her tuna *sambuus* were, and still are, the best. You'll sometimes find versions with a touch of shredded coconut, which works surprisingly well. I like it with *bisbaas qumbe* (see page 139) on the side. The tuna and coconut really bring out the best in each other. No matter what filling you choose, the most important thing is to keep it dry. Really dry. A wet filling can lead to soggy wrappers, torn corners, and leaks while frying… everything we don't want.

Sambuus *Samosas*

For the tuna filling

3 x 145-g/5-oz cans tuna in oil, drained
1 red onion, finely chopped
½ sweet (bell) pepper, green or red, finely chopped
2 green finger chillies (chiles), finely diced, seeds left in
2 spring onions (scallions), finely chopped
¼ tsp salt
¼ tsp ground cumin
juice of ½ lemon

For the tuna filling

If making the tuna filling, heat a frying pan (skillet) over medium-high heat and add the tuna. Cook for 6–8 minutes, stirring halfway through. The goal is to remove as much moisture as possible from the tuna without letting it become overly crispy or browned.

Add the onion and pepper to the pan and cook for another 6–8 minutes, stirring occasionally, until they release their moisture and the mixture is dry. Stir in the chillies and spring onions, mixing well, and cook for an additional 2 minutes.

Add the salt, cumin and freshly squeezed lemon juice. Stir again to combine and cook for a final 2 minutes before removing the pan from the heat. (If the tuna mixture still appears wet, continue cooking over medium heat for a few minutes more until it reaches a dry consistency.) Set the filling aside.

For the beef filling

250 g/9 oz minced (ground) beef
1 green finger chilli (chile), chopped, seeds left in
⅓ tsp ground coriander
½ tsp ground cumin
⅛ tsp ground black pepper
1 tsp salt
1 small onion, finely chopped
small handful fresh coriander (cilantro) leaves, finely chopped
small handful fresh dill, finely chopped (optional)
juice of ½ lemon

To assemble

2 tbsp plain (all-purpose) flour
12–15 samosa sheets (see pages 126–129 to make your own)
sunflower oil, for frying

For the beef filling

Place the minced beef in a frying pan (skillet) over medium–high heat. Cook for 10–12 minutes, using a wooden spoon or spatula to break the meat into small pieces as it cooks. Continue cooking until all the moisture evaporates and the meat becomes dry. Take care not to let the meat brown; the goal is to achieve a dry texture without caramelization.

Reduce the heat to medium, then stir in the chilli, ground coriander, ground cumin, black pepper and salt. Cook for another 2–3 minutes, allowing the spices to coat the meat evenly and release their aroma.

Add the onion, fresh coriander, fresh dill (if using) and lemon juice, mixing well to combine, then remove the pan from the heat. Set the filling aside.

To assemble and cook

Mix the flour with 2 tablespoons of water until you have a smooth paste. This will be the pastry glue.

To assemble to samosas, lay a triangular samosa sheet on a flat surface with the curved bottom edge closest to you. Fold the bottom edges inward, overlapping them slightly to form a pocket. Brush the overlapping edges with the pastry glue.

Press the edges gently to seal, creating a sturdy cone with an envelope-like opening at the top. Ensure the bottom and sides are securely sealed to prevent any filling from escaping during frying.

Take a spoonful of the filling, ensuring it's not too moist, and carefully spoon it into the cone. Be mindful not to overfill, as this can tear the pastry.

Brush the open edges at the top of the cone with pastry glue. Fold the top edge over to completely seal the samosa. Press firmly along the seams to ensure they are fully secured.

Repeat the process with the remaining pastry sheets and filling, keeping the prepared samosas covered with a damp kitchen towel to prevent them from drying out.

When ready to cook, heat oil in a deep frying pan (skillet) or pot over medium-high heat until it reaches 180°C/350°F, or until a cube of bread browns in 30 seconds. Fry the samosas in batches, cooking for 2–3 minutes on each side, until golden brown. Remove and place on a plate lined with paper towels to absorb any excess oil.

SERVES 12

This popular Somali snack is made by stuffing a boiled egg inside spiced mashed potato and frying until golden. The name derives from the Somali word for 'nutrition' or 'nourishment', and it's easy to see why. It's filling, comforting and satisfying. My version is slightly different, it skips the potato, uses only meat, and swaps chicken eggs for quail eggs, turning them into small, bite-sized snacks. Let me tell you, getting my family to try a quail egg was a moment. No one was convinced until my mum gave it her approval, stating the obvious that they taste exactly like chicken eggs. After that, quail eggs became our norm. You can use chicken eggs if you prefer, just double the filling ingredients.

Nafaqo *Scotch Eggs*

12 quail eggs
400 g/14 oz minced (ground) beef
½ tsp ground allspice
1 tsp garlic powder
1 tsp ground cumin
1 tsp paprika
½ tsp ground coriander
¾ tsp sumac
1 tsp salt
2 tbsp chopped parsley
70 g/2½ oz/½ cup plain (all-purpose) flour
2 eggs
20 g/¾ oz/½ cup panko breadcrumbs
sunflower oil, for frying

Begin by filling a small saucepan with water and bringing it to a boil. Gently lower the eggs into the boiling water and cook uncovered for 2 minutes 30 seconds for soft-boiled eggs, or 4 minutes for hard-boiled eggs. Prepare a bowl with ice-cold water. Once cooked, drain the eggs and transfer them to the cold water for 5 minutes to stop the cooking process. Carefully peel the eggs, being gentle as they are delicate, and set aside.

In a mixing bowl, combine the meat with the allspice, garlic powder, cumin, paprika, coriander, sumac and salt. Mix well to ensure the seasoning is evenly distributed, then divide the mixture into 12 equal balls.

Wet your hands and flatten each meatball into a patty. Sprinkle with parsley, then place a peeled egg in the centre. Carefully shape the meat around the egg, sealing it completely. Roll gently between your palms to form a smooth, even shape. Repeat with the remaining eggs and meat.

Set up three small bowls for coating. Place the flour in one, whisk the eggs in the second, and add the breadcrumbs to the third.

Take a prepared Scotch egg and roll it in the flour, then coat it in the whisked egg, and finally, roll it in the breadcrumbs. Repeat to coat all the Scotch eggs.

Heat oil in a small pan over medium–high heat until it reaches 170°C/340°F, or until a cube of bread browns in 30 seconds. Once hot, carefully fry the Scotch eggs in batches of 3–4 for about 5 minutes, or until they are golden brown and crispy.

Transfer to a plate lined with paper towels to absorb any excess oil.

SERVES 8–10

Shurbad exists across many cultures, especially in East Africa, the Middle East and North Africa. The word comes from the Arabic root *shariba*, meaning 'to drink', and it refers to something light and warming, often served at the start of a meal. The ingredients and methods vary across regions, but the feeling is the same. It's a dish that many, myself included, make only during Ramadan – something that feels tied to the rhythm of the month. This version is gently spiced and comforting. You can use chicken if you prefer, and it freezes well, so you can make it weeks in advance.

Shurbad *Lamb, Oat and Barley Soup*

500 g/1 lb 2 oz lamb shoulder on the bone, meat diced
2 vegetable stock pots
400-g/14-oz can finely chopped tomatoes
180 g/6 oz/1 cup pearl barley
4 tbsp rolled oats
½ tsp ground cumin
½ tsp ground coriander
½ tsp curry powder
5 tbsp olive or sunflower oil
½ large brown onion, chopped
4 garlic cloves
small bunch fresh coriander (cilantro)
lemon juice or apple cider vinegar, to serve (optional)

In a large deep pot, combine the lamb and stock pots with 2.5 litres/10 cups of water. Place the pot over medium–high heat and bring to a boil, then reduce the heat to medium–low and simmer uncovered for about 1 hour 30 minutes, or until the meat is tender.

Remove the meat from the pot and shred it into small pieces, discarding the bones. Return the shredded meat to the pot.

Add the chopped tomatoes and barley to the pot, stirring to combine. Allow the mixture to cook, uncovered, for 45 minutes over medium–low heat, stirring occasionally. Then, add the oats along with the cumin, coriander and curry powder, stirring to mix well. Cook for 20 minutes, then remove from the heat.

In a separate saucepan, heat the oil over medium heat. Add the onion and cook until browned.

Crush the garlic and fresh coriander together using a pestle and mortar and add to the oil and onion. Mix well and cook for another minute.

Carefully pour the hot oil mixture into the pot of soup, stirring immediately to combine. Simmer for a further 10 minutes.

Best served hot with a squeeze of fresh lemon juice or a teaspoon of apple cider vinegar on each portion.

Tip: This soup can be stored in the freezer for up to 3 months. To serve, just defrost, warm through and finish with a quick herb oil. Don't forget the vinegar or a squeeze of lemon to bring it all together.

IFTAR

SERVES 4

This recipe brings together two things I love: *oodkac*, traditionally made from small, diced pieces of preserved meat, similar to jerky; and hummus, which I could happily eat with almost anything. It's inspired by the idea of layering something soft with something rich. The hummus is smooth and simple. Perfect with some chopped vegetables or falafel, but topped with spiced beef, a drizzle of olive oil and some nuts, it becomes something more filling and special. Just don't use pre-cooked chickpeas. Soaking them takes a little time, but it's worth it, I promise.

Hummus with Spiced Beef

250 g/9 oz/1½ cups dried chickpeas
2 tsp bicarbonate of soda (baking soda)
1 garlic clove
2 ice cubes
75 g/2½ oz/⅓ cup tahini
⅓ tsp salt, plus ½ tsp
juice of 2½ small lemons
1 tbsp olive oil
250 g/9 oz sirloin steak, cut into 2-cm/¾-inch cubes
½ tsp coarse black pepper
½ tsp ground cumin
30 g/1 oz/¼ cup pine nuts
extra virgin olive oil, to drizzle
sumac, to garnish (optional)
sweet paprika, to garnish (optional)
fresh parsley, chopped, to garnish (optional)

Add the chickpeas to a large saucepan and cover with water. Stir in 1 teaspoon of bicarbonate of soda, cover and cook over low heat for 1 hour. Drain the water, then refill the saucepan with fresh water and add another teaspoon of bicarbonate of soda. Cook over low heat for another hour, or until the chickpeas are very soft. To check if they're ready, press a chickpea against a spoon – if it squashes smoothly without any resistance, the chickpeas are done. Drain the chickpeas and leave them to cool.

In a blender, combine the chickpeas, garlic and ice cubes. The ice helps to create a smooth, velvety finish. Blend until smooth. Add the tahini, ⅓ teaspoon of salt and the lemon juice, then continue blending until the mixture is creamy and velvety. Set aside.

Heat the olive oil in a frying pan (skillet) over high heat. When the oil is hot, add the meat, ensuring the pieces are spread apart. Let the meat cook undisturbed to achieve a browned, crispy exterior. Once one side is browned, season with the ½ teaspoon of salt, pepper and cumin, then flip the meat to cook the other side. Add the pine nuts and cook for another 2 minutes, stirring occasionally to coat everything evenly.

To serve, place a dollop of the hummus in the centre of a serving plate and, using the back of a spoon, gently swirl outward while spinning the plate to create an even layer. Add the meat and pine nuts to the centre of the hummus. Optionally, drizzle with extra virgin olive oil and garnish the edges with a sprinkle of paprika and sumac for added flavour and colour.

SERVES 4-6

This lentil soup, known simply as *addas*, is made from the most basic pantry ingredients, but somehow always tastes like more than the sum of its parts, and I've been enjoying it since I was little. In fact it was one of the first meals I weaned my daughter with once we introduced spices. It was only recently that my good friend from Algeria introduced me to the addition of *ras el hanout*, a North African spice blend. The spices used are those I am very familiar with in Somali cooking. The soup thickens beautifully by the next day, almost like a soft daal. I'll often serve it over rice, or gently loosen it on the stove with a splash of water and enjoy it as soup again.

Addas Soup *Lentil Soup*

2-3 tbsp olive oil
1 large onion, finely chopped
4-5 garlic cloves, crushed
1 large carrot, peeled and finely chopped
300 g/10½ oz/1⅔ cups red split lentils, rinsed
1 heaping tbsp vegetable bouillon powder
1 tbsp plus 1 tsp ground cumin,
1 tbsp plus 1 tsp ras el hanout (I use Sofra)
1 tsp salt
400 ml/1¾ cups coconut milk
large handful freshly chopped coriander (cilantro), plus extra to garnish
lemon slices, to serve

Start by heating the olive oil in a large saucepan. Add the onion and sauté for 3-4 minutes until translucent. Add the garlic, allowing it to soften slightly before adding the carrot. Stir everything together and let it sauté for 1-2 minutes.

Add the rinsed lentils and stir well. You might notice the mixture clumping up, but continue stirring. Add the bouillon, cumin, ras el hanout and salt. Cook over low heat, stirring occasionally, for 30 seconds. Add the coconut milk, 1.3 litres/5½ cups of water and the fresh coriander. Adjust the salt to taste, then cover the pan and leave the mixture to simmer on medium-low heat for 20 minutes.

Once simmered, half-blend the mixture with a stick blender to create a creamy texture while keeping some chunks intact. If needed, add more water at this stage, remembering to check the salt. Let it simmer for another 15 minutes. Garnish with extra coriander and lemon and serve hot.

SERVES 4

They might not be meat, but corn ribs are just as fun to eat. Seeing the way they curl up as they roast, there's something so satisfying about eating them. Slicing a whole corn cob lengthways can be tricky (and not the safest job). I snap the cob in half with my hands, then use a knife to cut each half into quarters. The corn roasts up beautifully with crisp, golden edges that almost taste fried. You can top them with whatever you like – some of my favourites include Parmesan, sugar or honey. Eat as is or serve with your favourite dipping sauce. They're always a hit with little ones and make a fun appetizer to add to the table.

Corn Ribs

2 corn on the cob
30 g/1 oz/2 tbsp butter, softened
2 tbsp Cajun seasoning
1 tsp granulated sugar

Begin by halving the corn cobs by hand; they should snap easily. Place the halves in a saucepan of boiling water over medium heat and simmer for 10 minutes to soften. Drain and rinse under cold water to cool.

Preheat an air fryer to 190°C/375°F or an oven to 190°C fan/210°C/425°F/gas mark 7.

Lay each cob half flat on a chopping board and carefully slice lengthways into ribs. Then cut each rib in half crossways to create 16 pieces.

In a bowl, combine the softened butter and Cajun seasoning into a smooth paste. Use a spoon to spread the mixture evenly over the corn ribs, pressing gently to coat. Arrange the ribs in an air fryer basket and cook for 10 minutes, or on a baking tray in the oven for 15–18 minutes until golden and fragrant (cook for longer if you'd like them crispier).

Finish with a light sprinkle of sugar before serving.

MAKES 10–14

There's something about sausage rolls that just feels a little fancy. Like you really took the time. They're the kind of thing that makes people pause and ask, 'Did you make these?' and maybe even wonder if it's some secret family recipe. It's not. I'm Somali. There's no world where my grandmother was making sausage rolls. But once you try these, you'll get it. They even win over the pickiest of eaters. I prepare a big batch, freeze them flat on a tray, then toss them into a freezer bag and just take out what I need. No fuss. No regrets. If you haven't made sausage rolls before what exactly have you been doing?

Sausage Rolls

400 g/14 oz minced (ground) beef
small handful fresh coriander (cilantro) leaves, chopped
2 spring onions (scallions), chopped
4 garlic cloves, crushed
50 g/1¾ oz/⅔ cup dried breadcrumbs
1 tsp Dijon mustard
1 tsp salt
½ tsp black pepper
3 tbsp Branston pickle (sweet pickle)
60 g/2 oz/⅔ cup grated Cheddar
1 egg
1 pre-rolled sheet of puff pastry
1 egg yolk, beaten
4 tbsp black and white sesame seeds

Equipment
baking tray, lined

In a large mixing bowl, combine the beef, coriander, spring onions, garlic, breadcrumbs, mustard, salt and pepper. Mix thoroughly. Add the pickle and grated cheese, gently mixing them in. Avoid overmixing, as this can lead to a dense, dry filling. Crack in the egg and give the mixture a final stir until just combined.

Preheat the oven to 180°C fan/200°C/400°F/gas mark 6.

Unroll the puff pastry sheet, leaving it on its paper sheet. Slice the pastry lengthways into two equal strips.

Divide the meat mixture into two portions. Place one portion along the centre of each pastry strip, then shape into a long, even log.

Fold the pastry edges over the meat to enclose the filling, pressing firmly to seal. Flip the pastry logs, so the seams are underneath. Using a sharp knife, cut each log into bite-sized pieces, about 3–4 cm/1½ inches in length.

Arrange the sausage rolls on the prepared baking tray, leaving space between them. Lightly score the tops of each roll with two small slits for ventilation. Brush the beaten egg yolk generously over the tops of the sausage rolls. Sprinkle sesame seeds evenly over each piece.

Bake in the preheated oven for 20–25 minutes, or until the pastry is golden, puffed and crisp.

Let the sausage rolls cool slightly before serving for the best texture and flavour. These can be enjoyed warm or at room temperature.

SERVES 3

It's hard to imagine a weekend without *fuul*: a comforting fava bean stew that's been a staple across North and East Africa and the Middle East for generations. This recipe is quick, easy and affordable – and incredibly forgiving. If, like me, you're practical and short on time most days, you can use canned beans for convenience. *Fuul* also lends itself to creative variations in toppings – whether you like a drizzle of olive oil and a squeeze of lemon, or a sprinkle of fresh herbs, there's a way to suit every taste. This is the kind of dish you can whip up early for suhoor or just before iftar.

Fuul Mudammas *Stewed Fava Beans with Eggs and Feta*

1 tbsp olive oil, plus extra to serve
1 small onion, finely chopped
1 small tomato, finely chopped
1 garlic clove, crushed
400-g/14-oz can ready-to-eat peeled fava beans (I use California Garden Secret Recipe), drained
3 eggs
small bunch fresh coriander (cilantro), chopped
2 tbsp crumbled feta (optional)
flatbreads, to serve

In a pan over medium-low heat, add the olive oil and onion. Sauté until softened, then add the tomato and garlic. Continue cooking until soft and fragrant, about 2–3 minutes. Add the canned beans, stirring to combine, and let the mixture heat through on low heat. Allow it to simmer gently for 5 minutes. If the beans you are using are whole, then crush about 70 per cent of the beans with the back of a fork. Cover and cook on low for another 2–3 minutes, then turn off the heat.

Place the eggs in a small pan and add water to cover. Bring to the boil and cook for 10–12 minutes (to lose the creaminess of the yolk). Drain, then transfer the eggs to cold water to cool. Peel and halve the eggs.

Transfer the cooked beans to a serving dish and top with a generous drizzle of olive oil, the freshly chopped coriander, crumbled feta and the boiled eggs. Serve with fresh flatbread.

Mini Chicken Patties

MAKES ABOUT 60

These chicken patties show up at least once a week in my kitchen during Ramadan. They're more like kebabs shaped into small, flat rounds that crisp beautifully in the pan while staying tender inside. I don't even need to think twice when making them. They're the kind of thing you fry up quickly before iftar, serve with *bisbaas*, or tuck into soft dinner rolls with whatever else is on the table. They are also perfect for throwing on the grill when the weather's warm. There's no fuss with them, which is why they've stuck. Just enough spice, always juicy, and somehow much more satisfying than they should be.

1½ onions, chopped
2 green finger chillies (chiles), tops removed, seeds left in
1½ kg/3 lb 5 oz minced (ground) chicken
1½ tbsp crushed garlic
1½ tbsp finely chopped ginger
bunch fresh coriander (cilantro), finely chopped
1 large tomato, finely chopped
sunflower oil, for frying
Mini dinner rolls, to serve (see page 131, optional)

For the seasoning
2 tsp bicarbonate of soda (baking soda)
1 tbsp ground cumin
2 tsp ground coriander
2 tsp sweet paprika
2½ tsp salt
1 tsp garam masala

In a blender, combine the onions and green chillies, blending until smooth. Use a muslin (cheesecloth) or sieve (strainer) to drain any excess moisture from the onion purée.

In a large bowl, mix the minced chicken, onion mixture, garlic, ginger and coriander thoroughly. Add all the seasoning ingredients and mix well, working the mixture well to ensure it is fully combined. Gently fold in the chopped tomato.

Heat a frying pan (skillet) with enough oil for shallow frying. Take a small portion of the mixture, flatten it, and fry to check the seasoning, adjusting the salt as needed. Keep a cup of water nearby to wet your hands as you work, which will help prevent sticking. For each patty, scoop about 35–40 g/1¼–1½ oz of the mixture, shape into a flat circle and carefully place it in the hot oil. Repeat until the pan is full. Fry without moving for 3–4 minutes, or until the bottom of the patties are golden brown, then flip and cook the other side until golden. When done, transfer to paper towels to absorb any excess oil. Repeat until all the mixture is shaped and fried.

Serve the patties on their own or with mini dinner rolls.

SERVES 4

This potato salad leans more Middle Eastern than classic, with no mayo in sight. It's dressed with olive oil, lemon and warm spices, then tossed with plenty of herbs. It's light, sharp and best served just slightly warm or at room temperature. The sharpness of the fresh garlic might seem strong to you at first, but I promise it settles as it sits. A good one to make ahead and even better over the next few days.

Potato Salad

1 kg/2 lb 4 oz salad potatoes
80 ml/⅓ cup olive oil
5 tbsp lemon juice (from 1 small lemon)
1 tsp ground cumin
1½ tsp salt, or to taste
½ tsp black pepper
pinch of ground allspice
¼ tsp ground coriander
4–5 garlic cloves, thinly sliced
bunch fresh parsley, finely chopped
handful fresh coriander (cilantro), finely chopped

Begin by cutting the potatoes in half and boiling them for about 15 minutes, or until fork-tender. Drain the potatoes and set them aside to cool.

In a large mixing bowl, whisk together the olive oil, lemon juice and spices. Taste and adjust the salt if needed. Add the sliced garlic to the mixture and let it sit for 10 minutes, allowing the flavours to meld and the garlic to soften.

While the garlic marinates, cut the cooled potato halves in half again, leaving smaller halves intact. Add the fresh herbs to the marinade, followed by the potatoes. Gently toss to ensure the potatoes are evenly coated.

This dish can be served warm or refrigerated to enjoy as a cold salad.

Once the fast is broken and prayer is complete, the table begins to fill again. There's something beautiful about this second sitting. The return to food after that quiet pause, when everyone gathers again with renewed energy and conversation begins to flow. This is when the main dishes are served, warm and generous, the heart of the evening meal.

In many homes, this is the moment people wait for all day. After the stillness of fasting and the lightness of those first bites, this part of iftar feels rich, grounding and complete. These dishes don't rush you, they invite you to take your time. They fill the room with their aroma, bring people together around shared plates and offer comfort after the long stretch of restraint.

Growing up, iftar mains were always a mix of the familiar and the special: fragrant rice, slow-cooked meats, hearty stews and platters that made their way to the table only during Ramadan. Even the way they were served felt intentional – big enough to share, always with enough for someone to have seconds, or to drop by unannounced. That spirit of abundance wasn't about extravagance, it was about hospitality, warmth and the quiet joy of feeding others.

One example is my Somali rice (see page 72). A dish that never leaves the table. It's the recipe that first introduced my cooking to so many, shared again and again, and made in kitchens across the world. It's still the most popular dish I've ever shared, and the one that means the most to me. I've made it countless times, and each time, it reminds me where all of this started.

Many of the recipes in this chapter carry that same feeling. There's simplicity in my cooking, that's been shaped by life. By busy days, work deadlines, and not always having the luxury of hours to spend in the kitchen. Over time, I've adjusted my methods to fit my real life, without ever compromising on flavour. Because food doesn't have to be complicated to be beautiful. It just has to be made with care.

This chapter is a collection of those main dishes, some passed down, some created in my own kitchen, all made to be shared. However you choose to serve them, I hope they bring a sense of fullness, not just to the plate, but to the evening itself.

SERVES 4-6

Bariis Somali is the recipe that first got people talking about my cooking. It's one of those dishes that makes me feel deeply connected to my roots. The flavours are layered and, like many Somali dishes, it brings together sweet and savoury in a way that just makes sense. I've simplified the method so it comes together in just 15 minutes, but none of the flavour is lost. It's usually served with meat, like *suqaar* or chicken, and don't forget the banana, a classic Somali pairing that rounds everything out. You have to try it.

Bariis Somali *Aromatic Somali Rice*

300 g/10½ oz/1½ cups basmati rice (I use sella basmati)
125 ml/½ cup sunflower oil
1 onion, half sliced and half finely chopped
1 tomato, finely chopped
1 chicken stock cube
1 tbsp ground cumin
1 small cinnamon stick
4–5 cardamom pods, crushed open
handful coriander (cilantro)
3–4 garlic cloves
70 g/2½ oz/½ cup sultanas (golden raisins)
¼ tsp red or orange food colouring

Start by bringing a pot of water to the boil for the rice. While waiting, wash the rice thoroughly until the water runs clear. Once the water is boiling, add the rice and parboil for 8-10 minutes, or until the grains are clear and cooked on the edges but still firm in the centre.

While the rice is parboiling, heat the sunflower oil in a large pot over medium heat. Add the sliced onion and fry until golden brown and crispy, being careful not to overcook. Remove the onions from the oil and drain on paper towels.

In the same pot, add the chopped onion to the remaining oil and cook until softened. Add the tomato, chicken stock cube, cumin, cinnamon stick and cardamom pods (count the pods in order to remove them later). Stir and cook for 4-5 minutes until the tomatoes break down and the mixture becomes fragrant.

Crush the fresh coriander and garlic together using a pestle and mortar, then add this mixture to the pot. Cook for another 2 minutes, then add 125 ml/½ cup of water to the mortar, rinsing it to capture any remaining flavour. Pour this into the pot and stir. Lower the heat, and leave to cook for 2-3 minutes.

Drain the rice and carefully layer it over the sauce in the pot, making sure not to mix the two. The rice should sit on top as a covering layer without fully blending into the sauce. Scatter the fried onions over the rice, then rinse the raisins in hot water to soften and arrange them on top. Dot the food colouring in one corner.

Cover the pot with a kitchen towel to absorb excess moisture, place the lid tightly on to trap the steam, and move the pot to the smallest burner. Cook on the lowest heat for 8-10 minutes.

When ready, turn off the heat and remove the lid. A small plume of steam should escape – this indicates the rice is perfectly cooked. Let the rice cool slightly before mixing, allowing the food colouring to set.

SERVES 4–6

Lamb chops always feel like a treat. This version is tenderized with kiwi, which works really quickly to soften the meat without changing the flavour. Once marinated, they cook fast and stay juicy with crisp edges and lots of flavour. I usually serve them with rice or something fresh on the side, but, honestly, they're good with anything.

Lamb Chops

500 g/1 lb 2 oz lamb chops
2–3 tbsp olive oil
4–5 garlic cloves, crushed
1 sprig mint, chopped
small handful fresh coriander (cilantro), finely chopped
1½ tbsp Turkish grill mix
1 tsp ground cumin
¼ tsp ground nutmeg
½ tsp salt
1 kiwi, peeled

Begin by washing the lamb chops thoroughly and pat them dry. Place the lamb in a large bowl, then add the oil, garlic, herbs, Turkish seasoning, spices and salt. Mix well, ensuring the lamb is evenly coated. Cover the bowl and refrigerate for at least 1 hour to marinate.

Thirty minutes before cooking, mash the kiwi and mix it into the marinated lamb. Let it sit until the lamb comes to room temperature, but no longer than 30 minutes, as the kiwi can over-tenderize the meat.

Heat a frying pan (skillet) over medium–high heat. Cook the lamb chops for 4–5 minutes on each side, adjusting the time for more char if desired. Serve immediately.

SERVES 4-6

This Egyptian-style macaroni béchamel sits somewhere between a lasagne and a pasta bake. Layers of pasta, spiced meat and creamy sauce, all baked until golden and set. It's usually made with a lighter hand on the béchamel, but I'll say it: that's where it loses people. Go heavier on the sauce. You won't regret it.

Macaroni Béchamel

500 g/1 lb 2 oz minced (ground) beef
90 ml/6 tbsp olive oil
1½ onions, finely chopped
4 garlic cloves
small handful fresh coriander (cilantro) leaves
1 tbsp tomato purée (paste)
1 tbsp pesto
400-g/14-oz can chopped tomatoes
1 tbsp chicken bouillon powder
¼ tsp ground nutmeg
½ tsp salt, plus extra if needed
2 tsp black pepper
200 g/7 oz penne pasta

For the béchamel
100 g/3½ oz/7 tbsp unsalted butter
100 g/3½ oz/scant ¾ cup plain (all-purpose) flour
1.1 litres/4½ cups milk (any milk will work)
pinch of salt
1 tsp chicken bouillon powder
1 tsp black pepper
½ tsp ground nutmeg
100 g/3½ oz/generous 1 cup pre-grated mozzarella
100 g/3½ oz/generous 1 cup grated Cheddar

Place a large saucepan over medium heat, add the minced beef and cook, breaking it down with a wooden spoon and allowing the liquid to cook off, for about 5 minutes. Add the olive oil and, once hot, add the onions, cooking for another 5 minutes until softened.

Using a pestle and mortar, crush the garlic and fresh coriander together, then add this mixture to the pan along with 2 tablespoons of water, stirring to combine. Stir in the tomato purée and pesto, followed by the chopped tomatoes, chicken bouillon, nutmeg, salt and pepper. Simmer for about 10 minutes. Adjust the salt if needed and leave to cool slightly.

Cook the pasta according to package instructions, then drain and leave in the pan.

In a separate saucepan, make the béchamel. Melt the butter over medium heat. Add the flour and stir vigorously until it reaches a smooth, batter-like consistency. Gradually pour in the milk, whisking continuously to avoid lumps. Continue whisking until the sauce thickens. Add the salt, bouillon powder, black pepper and nutmeg, stirring until the sauce becomes smooth and velvety. Remove from the heat and stir in half of the mozzarella and Cheddar cheeses until melted.

Preheat the oven to 180°C fan/200°C/400°F/gas mark 6.

In a large baking dish, combine the cooked pasta and meat sauce, mixing to coat the pasta evenly. Spread half of the remaining cheese over the pasta mixture. Pour the béchamel sauce evenly over the top, followed by the remaining cheese.

Cover the dish with foil and bake for 35 minutes. Remove the foil, switch on the grill (broiler) and cook for another 5 minutes until the top is golden brown.

SERVES 6–8

Bisteeki, also commonly known as *buskeeti*, is a classic Somali steak dish. It's known for how thinly the meat is sliced and how tender it becomes once cooked. This recipe is, in fact, my older sister's. She uses milk to tenderize the meat and soy sauce to give a rich umami flavour, which isn't typical in a Somali kitchen, but it works. If possible, try to source the meat from a Somali butcher, as it's already thinly sliced and will cook more quickly. If not, you can bash it lightly to get the same result.

Bisteeki *Thinly Sliced Spiced Steak*

1 kg/2 lb 4 oz very thin beef steaks, cut with a meat slicer
125 ml/½ cup milk (it needs to be cow's milk)
4 tbsp olive oil
1 small onion, cut into wedges or thick slices
1 (bell) pepper, thickly sliced
1 tomato, cut into wedges or thick slices
½ tsp Vegeta or all-purpose seasoning or salt
30 g/ 1 oz / 2 tbsp unsalted butter
1 tbsp light soy sauce
1 tsp dark soy sauce
4–5 garlic cloves
4 tbsp coriander (cilantro) leaves

For the bisteeki seasoning
1½ tsp ground cumin
1 tsp salt
1 tsp ground black pepper
½ tsp sweet paprika
½ tsp smoked paprika
½ tsp garlic powder
¼ tsp onion powder
½ tsp cayenne pepper
½ tsp dried rosemary or oregano
½ tsp Vegeta or all-purpose seasoning

Put the steak in a mixing bowl and pour the milk over, ensuring the meat is fully submerged. Let it sit for 10 minutes while you prepare the seasoning. This step helps tenderize the meat.

In a separate bowl, combine all the ingredients for the bisteeki seasoning and mix thoroughly.

After marinating, strain the steak, discarding the milk. Sprinkle over the beef seasoning and drizzle with 2 tablespoons of olive oil. Use your hands to mix well, ensuring the steak is evenly coated.

Heat a frying pan (skillet) over medium heat and add the remaining 2 tablespoons of olive oil. When hot, add the onion, pepper and tomato along with the Vegeta or salt. Stir and sauté for 3–4 minutes until the vegetables are cooked but still retain a slight bite. Transfer to a plate and set aside.

Use the same frying pan to cook the steaks, working in batches to avoid overcrowding the pan. Place 1–2 pieces of steak in the pan at a time and sear for 1 minute on each side until browned. Repeat with the remaining steaks.

In the same frying pan, add the butter, light soy sauce and dark soy sauce. Allow the mixture to simmer for 2 minutes, stirring occasionally, until the butter has melted and the sauce begins to bubble gently.

Using a pestle and mortar, crush the garlic and coriander into a coarse paste. Add this to the pan, stirring to combine. Pour 2 tablespoons of water into the mortar to rinse out any remaining paste and add it to the pan. Mix well and reduce the heat to low.

Add all the cooked steaks back into the pan, turning the pieces over a few times to coat the steaks lightly with the sauce. Leave to cook over low heat for 1–2 minutes.

Serve hot, topped with the sautéed vegetables.

SERVES 6-8

This is a variation of my usual *bisteeki* (see page 79), but with a crumb coating that adds a lovely texture. My paternal aunt made it for me years ago, and it's stuck with me ever since. I don't make it as often, but when I do, I'm reminded of how much I love it. It's not something you see all the time – breaded steak isn't the most common dish, which makes it feel a little special when it does appear. I keep it warm in a low oven to stop the coating from softening, and I always wait to add the tomato salad until just before serving so everything stays crisp and fresh.

Breaded Bisteeki with Tomato Salad

1 kg/2 lb 4 oz very thin beef steaks, cut with a meat slicer
125 ml/½ cup milk (it needs to be cow's milk)
1 quantity of bisteeki seasoning (see page 79)
225 g/8 oz/3 cups fine dried breadcrumbs
3 eggs
200 ml/1 scant cup sunflower oil
1 kg/2 lb 4 oz tomatoes
1 small white onion
60 ml/¼ cup olive oil
1 large garlic clove, crushed
½ tsp salt
¼ tsp ground black pepper
4 tbsp chopped parsley

Put the steak in a mixing bowl and pour the milk over, ensuring the meat is fully submerged. Let it sit for 10 minutes while you prepare the seasoning. This step helps tenderize the meat.

In a separate bowl, combine all the ingredients for the bisteeki seasoning and mix thoroughly.

After marinating, strain the steak, discarding the milk. Pat the steaks dry with paper towels to remove any excess liquid, as the meat needs to be as dry as possible. Set aside ½ teaspoon of the beef seasoning and sprinkle the rest evenly over the steaks, ensuring each piece is well coated.

On a plate, mix the breadcrumbs with the reserved ½ teaspoon of seasoning. In a separate shallow dish, beat the eggs until smooth.

Preheat the oven to 180°C fan/200°C/400°F/gas mark 6.

Heat the sunflower oil in a shallow frying pan (skillet) over medium heat until it reaches 180°C/350°F, or until a cube of bread browns in 30 seconds. Working with one piece of steak at a time, dip it into the beaten eggs, then coat it in the breadcrumbs. Ensure it is evenly coated, pressing down if needed. Place the breaded steak on a plate or wire rack and repeat the process with the remaining pieces.

When the oil is hot, fry the steaks for about 2 minutes on each side, or until golden brown. Be careful not to overcrowd the pan, as this will lower the oil temperature. Once fried, transfer the steaks to a plate lined with paper towels to absorb any excess oil.

To ensure the breaded coating remains firmly adhered, transfer the fried steak to a baking sheet (the pieces can slightly overlap if necessary) and bake in the preheated oven for 15 minutes.

Meanwhile, slice the tomatoes into wedges and thinly slice the onions. Put them in a large mixing bowl.

In a smaller bowl, whisk together the olive oil, garlic, salt, pepper and most of the parsley. Pour this mixture over the tomatoes and onions, and toss gently to combine. Let the salad sit for a few minutes to marinate, allowing the flavours to meld. Sprinkle with the rest of the parsley and give it one final toss.

When ready to serve, spoon the tomato salad over the steaks. Be sure to do this just before serving, as the tomato juices can soften the coating if added too early.

SERVES 4

This is my mum's cheat version of *maqlooba*, a traditional dish from the Levant, which simply means 'upside down' in Arabic – because that's exactly how it's served. It's not trying to be the original, just something simpler that captures the same spirit. The only thing it really shares is the method: meat at the bottom, then vegetables, then rice, all flipped before serving. But it comes together quickly and still delivers all the comfort you'd expect from a dish like this. It takes hardly any time to make, but still feels like something special. There's an ongoing joke in my family that my version has officially outdone my mum's – and in any household, that's saying something!

Upside-Down Chicken Rice

300 g/10½ oz/1½ cups basmati rice (I use sella basmati)

½ tsp salt

4 chicken skinless thighs, bone in

1 potato, peeled and cut into large chips

1 carrot, peeled and cut into large chips

1 large onion, cut into large rings

2 (bell) peppers (different colours), cut into thick rings

60 ml/¼ cup olive or sunflower oil

For the chicken seasoning

1 tbsp ground cumin

1 tbsp ground coriander

1 tsp chicken or vegetable seasoning

¼ tsp ground turmeric

For the vegetable seasoning

¼ tsp ground turmeric

1 tsp ground cumin

1 tsp ground coriander

1 tsp chicken bouillon powder

Begin with placing the rice in a bowl with the salt and cover it with boiling water. Soak for 30 minutes to soften the grains and remove excess starch. After soaking, rinse the rice thoroughly several times until the water runs clear, then drain well.

Wash the chicken and season it with the chicken seasoning ingredients. Place the chicken in a deep pot, arranging it with the bone side facing up to help the meat cook evenly.

Layer the potato and carrot over the chicken first, followed by the onion rings. Sprinkle the turmeric evenly over the vegetables, then arrange the pepper rings on top. Sprinkle the remaining vegetable seasoning ingredients evenly across the top. Avoid mixing to maintain the distinct layers.

Add the drained rice, spreading it evenly over the vegetables to cover them completely. It's fine if some vegetables peek through. Drizzle the oil over the rice to prevent sticking.

Cover the pot with a clean kitchen towel to absorb excess moisture, then secure the lid tightly on top. Place the pot over high heat and cook for 8 minutes to lightly brown the chicken and bring the pot to temperature. Move the pot to the smallest burner and set to the lowest heat. Cook for 40 minutes, or until the potatoes and carrots are tender and the rice is fully cooked.

To serve, gently scoop out the contents from the bottom up, ensuring the layers remain intact.

SERVES 6-8

Falafel is loved across the Middle East, and while its origin is still up for debate, one thing's certain: everyone swears their version is the best. I won't get involved in that argument, but I will say this: you should try this one and decide for yourself. I add a little potato to the mix – absolutely not traditional, I know, but it gives the falafel a softer middle while still keeping that golden crisp outside. Some may call it unorthodox, I call it delicious. It's not as intimidating as it looks, and the results are golden, crisp and full of flavour. Just don't reach for canned chickpeas. Soaked dried chickpeas are essential if you want the texture just right.

Falafel

340 g/12 oz/2 cups dried chickpeas
½ tsp bicarbonate of soda (baking soda)
small handful fresh parsley
small handful fresh coriander (cilantro)
1 small potato, peeled and halved
1 small onion, halved
8 garlic cloves
1 tsp salt
1 tbsp ground cumin
1 tbsp ground coriander
1 tbsp black pepper
1 tsp baking powder
sunflower oil, for frying

Start by placing the dried chickpeas in a bowl and cover them with water. Ensure the chickpeas are fully immersed as they will expand. Stir in the bicarbonate soda, cover and leave to rest for 8–24 hours.

Once soaked, drain and rinse the chickpeas, then pat them dry as much as possible.

In a blender, combine the chickpeas, parsley, fresh coriander, potato, onion, garlic, salt and spices. Blend in 30-second intervals until the mixture is finely processed. Transfer the mixture to a bowl and refrigerate for at least 1 hour.

When ready to cook, stir in the baking powder. Take a couple of tablespoons of the mixture and form it into a small patty about 1 cm/½ inch thick using wet hands, a falafel tool or a small ice cream scoop. Repeat to shape all the mixture into patties.

Heat the oil in a pan until it reaches 180°C/350°F, or until a cube of bread browns in 30 seconds. Working in batches, carefully drop the patties into the hot oil and cook for 5–7 minutes, turning occasionally, until golden brown and crispy. Be careful not to overcrowd the pan.

As the falafels cook, place the finished ones in a colander lined with paper towels to absorb the excess oil. Serve the falafel hot.

SERVES 4

Suqaar has always been a constant. It's one of the first dishes I learned to make. It is quick, reliable, and something you can always build a meal around. The word itself comes from the idea of cutting things small, which is exactly what it is: small pieces of meat cooked down with onions, a few spices and vegetables. It's great in that it works with any meat, which makes it easy to come back to. It pairs beautifully with *laxoox* (see page 117) or *malawax* (see page 120).

Suqaar *Diced Beef and Vegetable Sauté*

400 g/14 oz chuck or stewing beef, diced into 1-cm/½-inch cubes
60 ml/¼ cup sunflower oil
1 tbsp Xawaash (see page 142)
1 vegetable stock pot
1 tsp ground cumin
1 tbsp sweet paprika
1 tsp tamarind paste
1 onion, finely chopped
1 tomato, finely chopped
small handful fresh coriander (cilantro) leaves
3–4 garlic cloves
1 small (bell) pepper, green or red, sliced or finely chopped
Shidni (see page 138), to serve

Begin by washing and rinsing the beef thoroughly. Place the beef in a large frying pan and add the oil, xawaash, vegetable stock pot, cumin and paprika. Set the heat to medium and mix well to coat the beef evenly. Cook for about 20 minutes, allowing the beef to release its natural juices and create a gravy.

Stir in the tamarind, mix thoroughly, cover with a lid, and cook for another 20 minutes. Remove the lid, then add the onion and tomato. Cook until the onion softens – about 10 minutes.

Crush the fresh coriander and garlic and add to the pan, mixing well. Lower the heat and simmer for an additional 20 minutes until the meat is tender.

Turn off the heat and scatter the pepper over the dish. Cover the pan and let the residual heat soften the pepper before serving with shidni.

SERVES 4

Cod is one of my favourite fish. It's incredibly quick to cook and mild in flavour. This recipe feels like you've made an effort, but really, it comes together with very little fuss. The fish is coated in flour, dipped in egg and shallow-fried in a mix of ghee and olive oil until golden. Then, because we're not letting all that flavour go to waste, I use the same pan to make a quick herby sauce to pour over the top. It's the kind of dish that looks like you had a plan, even if you didn't.

Pan-Fried Cod

2 skinless and boneless cod loins
70 g / 2½ oz / ½ cup plain (all-purpose) flour
¾ tsp salt
¾ tsp black pepper
¼ tsp ground cumin
1 egg
3 tbsp ghee
1 tbsp olive oil
juice of ½ lemon
4 tbsp chopped parsley

Cut the cod into four even pieces and pat them dry thoroughly with paper towels to remove excess moisture; this helps the coating stick better and ensures even frying.

In a shallow bowl, combine the flour with the salt, pepper and cumin, mixing well to season evenly. In a separate shallow bowl, beat the egg until smooth.

Heat the ghee and olive oil in a frying pan (skillet) over medium-high heat until hot but not smoking. To check, you can drop a small piece of the flour mixture into the oil; if it sizzles gently, the oil is ready.

Dredge each piece of cod in the seasoned flour, ensuring it's fully coated, then dip into the beaten egg, allowing any excess to drip off. Place the coated fish carefully into the hot pan and cook for 3–4 minutes on each side until golden brown and cooked through. Once cooked, remove the fish from the pan and transfer to a plate.

Lower the heat to low, add the lemon juice to the pan, and let it simmer for about 30 seconds, stirring to combine. Add the parsley, stir briefly, and pour the sauce over the cooked fish.

MAKES 8-10 PIECES

If you're going to make fried chicken at home, it might as well be worth the effort. This version is exactly that: the kind of chicken that crackles as you bite in, with a crust full of spice and texture, and meat that stays juicy all the way through. I season both the marinade and the flour, because what's the point if the flavour's only on the outside? And the best part? You didn't pick it up from a shop or spend a fortune. This is all you! Served in dinner rolls (see page 131) as burgers or in a big basket for everyone to tuck into, it's the kind of thing people won't stop reaching for.

Fried Chicken

about 1.4 kg/3 lb 2 oz boneless skin-on chicken thighs
groundnut (peanut), rapeseed (canola) oil or sunflower oil, for frying
salt

For the wet mix
500 ml/2 cups buttermilk
1 tsp garlic powder
1 tsp sweet paprika
1 tsp cayenne pepper
1 tsp black pepper
1 tsp salt

For the dry mix
280 g/10 oz/2 cups plain (all-purpose) flour
100 g/3½ oz/1 cup cornflour (cornstarch)
1½ tsp salt
1 tsp garlic powder
1 tsp sweet paprika
1 tsp cayenne pepper
1 tsp black pepper

Place the chicken in a bowl and add the wet mix ingredients. Mix thoroughly to coat the chicken, then cover and marinate overnight. This step is crucial for tender and flavourful chicken.

When ready to fry, remove the chicken from the fridge at least 30 minutes beforehand to bring it to room temperature.

In a separate bowl, combine the dry mix ingredients and add 2-3 tablespoons of the wet mix. Stir well to create a crumbly texture. Take one piece of chicken at a time and press it firmly into the dry mixture, ensuring it is fully and evenly coated for a crispy finish. Place the coated chicken on a wire rack and repeat to coat the remaining pieces.

Add enough oil to a deep pan to fully submerge the chicken and heat to 185°C/365°F. Test the temperature by dipping the back of a wooden spoon or chopstick into the oil – if it sizzles, the oil is ready. Carefully add 3–4 pieces of chicken at a time, ensuring the pan is not overcrowded. Avoid touching the chicken while frying to prevent the coating from sticking or breaking.

Fry the chicken for 7-8 minutes on each side, or until it is golden brown and cooked through. Transfer the cooked chicken to a wire rack lined with paper towels to drain any excess oil. Lightly sprinkle with salt while hot to enhance the flavour, then serve immediately.

SERVES 4

If you are Somali, you either love *soor* or you don't. I've always felt that those who don't just haven't had it with the right consistency or with the right stew. It shouldn't be as thick or dense as *ugali* or *fufu*, and it's not as soft as porridge – it sits somewhere perfectly in-between. When made right, it's incredibly comforting. Oxtail isn't something I grew up eating; I was introduced to it later and completely fell for it. When it's cooked properly and falling off the bone, there's nothing like it. The flavours in this dish are mostly Somali, but with a little twist I picked up from a close Jamaican friend – she adds ketchup, and I've never looked back. Don't skip it.

Oxtail Stew with Soor *Oxtail Stew with Grits*

700 g/1 lb 9 oz oxtail
1 tbsp white vinegar
6 spring onions (scallions)
small bunch thyme
3 tbsp sunflower oil
1½ tbsp Worcestershire sauce
2 tbsp tomato ketchup
1 tbsp date paste
1 large carrot
1 small onion
6 garlic cloves
2 tsp fine onion gravy powder
1 tsp xawaash (see page 142)
1 tsp salt
¾ tsp vegetable seasoning
2 bay leaves
4 cardamom pods, crushed

For the soor
500 ml/2 cups coconut milk
1 tsp Vegeta or all-purpose seasoning or salt
350 g/12 oz/2 cups semolina

Start by placing the oxtail in a large bowl and adding the vinegar. Mix thoroughly to clean, then rinse under cold water and drain any excess. Transfer the oxtail to a large pot along with four of the spring onions, thyme and 700 ml/3 cups of water. Cover and simmer on medium–low heat for 1 hour 30 minutes.

Once cooked, strain the oxtail, reserving the stock but discarding the thyme and spring onions.

In the same pot, heat the oil over medium–high heat. Add the oxtail along with the Worcestershire sauce, ketchup and date paste. Cook for about 5 minutes, allowing the meat to brown evenly.

While the oxtail browns, prepare the vegetables. In a blender, combine the carrot, onion, garlic and the remaining two spring onions. Blend into a coarse paste with a sand-like texture.

Remove the oxtail from the pot and set it aside on a plate. Add the blended vegetables to the pot and cook the vegetables over medium heat, stirring occasionally, for 8–10 minutes until they soften and release their aroma. Return the oxtail to the pot, then sprinkle in the gravy powder, xawaash, salt and vegetable seasoning. Stir well to combine.

Pour 500 ml/2 cups of the reserved stock back into the pot (adding more water if needed to reach this amount) and add the bay leaves and crushed cardamom pods. Stir and bring to a simmer over medium–high heat for 10 minutes.

Reduce the heat to low, cover with a lid and cook for 60 minutes. The cardamom pods should rise to the surface – remove them at this stage.

Preheat the oven to 180°C fan/200°C/400°F/gas mark 6.

Transfer the pot to the oven and continue to cook for 1 hour–1 hour 30 minutes, or until the meat is tender and falling off the bone and the sauce has a rich stew-like consistency. If it becomes too thick, add a little water to loosen it. Remove the bay leaves.

For the soor, in a large pan, combine the coconut milk and 1.25 litres/5 cups water over medium heat. Stir in the Vegeta and heat the mixture until it's hot but not yet boiling. Gradually add the semolina while continuously stirring to prevent lumps. Keep stirring until it forms a smooth paste. Once combined, reduce the heat to low, cover the pan, and let it cook for 20–25 minutes, stirring occasionally to ensure it doesn't stick. The soor should be thick yet still easy to mix.

When ready, plate the soor and serve the oxtail in the centre.

Tip: The *soor* can also be served with *suugo sabaayad* (see page 97).

SERVE 4–5

Isku karis means 'to cook with', and *baasto* means 'pasta', so the name refers to the pasta simmered in the stew, rather than cooked on the side like you might expect. It's usually made with red meat and short-cut pasta, and it's the kind of meal that settles you. It's familiar, full and deeply satisfying. I have core memories of eating this at my mum's friend's house and coming home to request it constantly. Coconut isn't usually a part of this dish, but in Southern Somali cooking, there's a dish called *kalamudo* that often includes it. The sweetness works so well with the richness of the stew. I usually use my *bisbaas qumbe* as the coconut element in this dish. It adds a subtle heat, and I always serve more on the side.

Baasto Isku Karis *One-Pot Lamb Pasta*

400 g/14 oz lamb shoulder on the bone, meat diced
bunch fresh coriander (cilantro)
5 tbsp sunflower oil
3–5 garlic cloves
2 tsp xawaash (see page 142)
1 tbsp tomato purée (paste)
½ tsp tamarind paste
1 green chilli (chile), top removed, seeds left in
1 onion, finely chopped
3 salad tomatoes, blended until smooth
1 chicken stock cube
40 g/1½ oz/½ cup desiccated (dried unsweetened shredded) coconut, or 2 tbsp bisbaas qumbe (see page 139), or to taste
250 g/9 oz dried pasta
1 tsp Vegeta or all-purpose seasoning
salt, to taste
juice of ½ lemon

Begin by washing the lamb thoroughly under cold water. Place the lamb in a large, heavy-bottomed pan along with the one-quarter of the fresh coriander. Pour in about 1 litre/4 cups of water, or enough to cover the meat completely. Cover the pan with a lid, set the heat to medium–low and let the meat simmer gently for 40 minutes to tenderize.

After 40 minutes, carefully drain the liquid from the pan, leaving the lamb behind and reserving the stock for later.

Add the oil to the pan and heat over medium heat. Brown the lamb on all sides. Crush the garlic and half of the remaining coriander using a pestle and mortar, then add to the pan. Add the xawaash, tomato purée, tamarind paste and green chilli, stirring to coat the meat. Cook for 2–3 minutes to develop the flavours.

Add the onion and cook until caramelized and the oil rises to the top. Pour in the blended tomatoes, stirring well to coat the meat evenly. Pour 3 tablespoons of water into the mortar to gather any leftover flavours, then add this to the pan. Add the reserved stock (about 700 ml/3 cups), the stock cube and the coconut or bisbaas qumbe and stir well.

Add the pasta, stirring it into the sauce so it's fully submerged. If the mixture appears too thick, add a little hot water as needed until the pasta is covered. Add the Vegeta seasoning and, if needed, salt to taste. Cover the pan and cook for 10–11 minutes, or until the pasta is al dente or cooked to your preference.

Once the pasta is done, remove the pan from the heat. Squeeze in the lemon juice, add a little of the remaining coriander and, if desired, add a spoonful of bisbaas qumbe. Give it a stir and serve immediately, garnished with the rest of the coriander.

SERVES 4–6

This is a slow-cooked, roasted stew that's rich, deeply spiced and made to be scooped up with *sabaayad*, also known as *kimis*. The bread catches every bit of the sauce, which is exactly what makes it so satisfying. I genuinely loved coming home from school to find my mum had made it, and it almost always meant *sabaayad* was on the side too. A labour of love, and it tasted like it.

It's not just for *sabaayad*, though. You can have it with *laxoox* (see page 117), *muufo* (see page 119) or even with regular pasta or rice. It holds up beautifully either way.

Suugo Sabaayad *Lamb Stew*

500 g/1 lb 2 oz lamb shoulder on the bone, meat diced
large handful fresh coriander (cilantro), roughly chopped, plus extra to garnish
2–3 tbsp sunflower oil
1 large onion, finely chopped
4–5 garlic cloves, crushed
1 tbsp tomato purée (paste)
1 tbsp chicken bouillon powder
1 tbsp onion gravy powder
1 tbsp sweet paprika
1 tbsp ground cumin
1 tbsp ground coriander
1½ tsp salt
1 large potato, peeled and cut into 2.5-cm/1-inch cubes
1 large carrot, peeled and cut into 2-cm/¾-inch cubes
400-g/14-oz can chopped tomatoes
Kimis (see page 123), flatbread or rice, to serve

In a large pot, add the lamb shoulder, 700 ml/3 cups of water and the chopped coriander. Cover and bring to the boil over medium heat, and cook until the lamb is just tender – about 40 minutes.

Once the meat has softened, uncover the pot and ladle out the broth into a large bowl or container (reserving the broth for later use). Add the vegetable oil to the pot and fry the lamb until it's lightly browned. If needed, you can use some of the reserved broth in place of oil.

Add the onion and garlic to the meat, frying until the onion turns translucent. If the pan seems too dry, stir in a little more of the broth. Add the tomato purée and stir to combine. Stir in the chicken bouillon, onion gravy powder, paprika, cumin, ground coriander and salt. Mix well, ensuring the spices coat the meat evenly. Add the potato, carrot, chopped tomatoes and 500-550 ml/2-2¼ cups of the reserved broth (make the quantity up with hot water, if you do not have enough broth). Combine thoroughly.

Cover the pot and simmer on low heat for 40–60 minutes, allowing the stew to thicken and the vegetables to soften. Again, if needed, add more broth. For a thicker sauce, cook uncovered for a few extra minutes. Serve with kimis, flatbread or rice.

SERVES 2

A couple of years ago, I was on a boat in Egypt when I was served the most incredible sea bass, grilled fresh, straight off the fire. I asked for the recipe, of course, but got the usual vague replies: a bit of this, a bit of that. So I went home and did what I could to piece it together. This version is what came from that, and it's stayed with me ever since. It's simple, packs a flavour punch and is the kind of dish that doesn't need much else.

Grilled Sea Bass

1 whole sea bass, gutted, deboned and butterflied (you can ask your fishmonger to do this)
2 tsp salt
handful fresh coriander (cilantro)
5 garlic cloves
1 tomato
1 red (bell) pepper
1 green finger chilli (chile), top removed, seeds left in
¾ tsp sweet paprika
1 tsp ground cumin
1 tsp ground coriander
3 tbsp lemon juice, plus extra to serve
3 tbsp olive oil

For the topping
1 tbsp olive oil
1 small onion, thinly sliced
1 carrot, peeled and finely grated
1 red romano (bell) pepper, thinly sliced

Start by thoroughly washing the fish and placing it on a baking sheet. Rub 1 teaspoon of the salt onto the skin, then turn the butterflied fish skin-side down.

In a blender, combine the fresh coriander, garlic, tomato, red pepper and green chilli. Blend until smooth, then add the paprika, cumin, ground coriander and remaining 1 teaspoon of salt. Mix well to combine. Taste the mixture, adjusting the salt if needed. Stir in the lemon juice and olive oil until well mixed.

Rub the sauce all over the fish and refrigerate for 20 minutes.

Meanwhile, preheat the oven to 220°C fan/240°C/475°F/gas mark 9.

Place the fish in the preheated oven and bake for 10 minutes.

While the fish cooks, prepare the topping. Heat the olive oil in a frying pan (skillet) and add the sliced onion, carrot and red pepper. Sauté for 3-4 minutes, keeping the vegetables slightly crisp.

Remove the fish from the oven and add the sautéed vegetables on top. Move the baking sheet to the top oven shelf, turn on the grill (broiler) and cook until the vegetables are lightly charred – about 5 minutes.

Remove from the oven and drizzle with extra lemon juice before serving.

SERVES 4

I know the word 'curry' can sometimes feel intimidating, like it's going to be complicated, full of hard-to-find spices or require more effort than you have time for. But this isn't one of those recipes (I promise). This coconut curry is as straightforward as they come, made with simple, everyday ingredients you can find in almost any kitchen. It's proof that you don't need much to create something full of depth and warmth.

Coconut Chicken Curry

300 g/10½ oz boneless chicken thighs or breast
1 tsp sweet paprika
½ tsp ground turmeric
1 tsp salt
60 ml/¼ cup sunflower oil
1 large onion, finely chopped
4 garlic cloves
1 bay leaf
160 ml/⅔ cup coconut cream
1½ tsp ground cumin
1½ tsp curry powder
1½ tsp Vegeta or all-purpose seasoning
½ x 400-g/14-oz can chopped tomatoes
2 tsp brown sugar
1 tsp cayenne pepper
chopped fresh coriander (cilantro), to serve
lime juice, to serve

Begin by trimming any excess fat from the chicken and cutting it into 2.5-cm/ 1-inch pieces. Place the chicken in a bowl and add the paprika, turmeric and salt. Mix well and set aside to marinate for 20 minutes while preparing the remaining ingredients.

In a large pot, heat the oil over medium heat. Add the onion and cook, stirring occasionally, for 10–12 minutes until the onion has softened and is glossy. Add the garlic and cook for 2–3 minutes. Stir until the moisture from the onion has evaporated.

Add the chicken and bay leaf to the pot, stirring well to coat. Pour in the coconut cream and cook for 2–3 minutes, allowing it to coat the chicken and come to a gentle boil. Add the cumin, curry powder and Vegeta and stir well. Add the chopped tomatoes and brown sugar. Stir well to combine, then lower the heat and simmer for 15 minutes.

Stir in 80 ml/⅓ cup of water and bring the curry to the boil, then reduce the heat and let it simmer on low for 30–40 minutes, or until the chicken is tender and the oil rises to the surface. Stir in the cayenne, then turn off the heat and allow the curry to sit for a few minutes to enhance the flavours.

Reheat gently before serving, adjusting the salt if needed. Serve with freshly chopped coriander and a squeeze of fresh lime juice.

SERVES 8

Slow roasting in the oven brings out the best in the vegetables here – deep, rich and slightly sweet. This is exactly the kind of lasagne I love: hot, messy and spooned straight from the dish. But if you're after clean layers and a neater slice, let it rest for at least 30 minutes before serving.

This dish can be prepped ahead and frozen, and it's a great way to get in more vegetables, especially for anyone in the family who'd normally protest. You can swap the vegetables depending on what's in season or what's in your fridge.

Roasted Vegetable Lasagne

1 aubergine (eggplant)
1 courgette (zucchini)
2 carrots
250 g/9 oz cherry tomatoes
1 red (bell) pepper
1 red onion
1 bulb of garlic
2–3 tbsp olive oil
2 tsp salt
690 g/1 lb 8 oz passata (strained tomatoes)
¼ tsp ground nutmeg
2 tbsp honey
1 vegetable stock cube
12–14 lasagne sheets
100 g/3½ oz/generous 1 cup pre-grated mozzarella
100 g/3½ oz/generous 1 cup grated Cheddar

For the béchamel
80 g/2¾ oz/5½ tbsp unsalted butter
80 g/2¾ oz/½ cup plus 2 tbsp plain (all-purpose) flour
1 litre/4 cups milk (any milk will work)
½ tsp salt
½ tsp vegetable bouillon powder
½ tsp black pepper
½ tsp ground nutmeg

Equipment
32 x 22-cm/13 x 9-inch baking dish

Preheat the oven to 180°C fan/200°C/400°F/gas mark 6.

Arrange the aubergine, courgette and carrots on a baking tray, along with the cherry tomatoes, red pepper, onion and garlic bulb. Drizzle over the olive oil, sprinkle with the salt and toss to coat evenly. Roast in the preheated oven for 45 minutes.

Once roasted, transfer the tomatoes, pepper (skin intact), onion and garlic (squeezed from the skins) into a blender and pulse until smooth. Pour the blended mixture into a saucepan, then stir in the passata, nutmeg, honey and stock cube. Mix well, add 125 ml/½ cup of water, and simmer over low heat for 30 minutes. Add the remaining roasted vegetables to the sauce and cook for a further 10 minutes.

To make the béchamel, melt the butter in a saucepan over medium heat. Add the flour and stir until smooth. Gradually pour in the milk, whisking continuously to prevent lumps. Keep whisking until the sauce thickens. Stir in the salt, bouillon powder, black pepper and nutmeg, ensuring the sauce is smooth and velvety. Remove from the heat.

Preheat the oven to 170°C fan/190°C/375°F/gas mark 5.

To assemble, start with a layer of béchamel in the baking dish, followed by lasagna sheets, then vegetable sauce and a small sprinkle of cheese. Repeat this pattern, alternating layers, until you reach the top, creating 4–5 layers. For the final layer, spread the remaining white sauce and a little tomato sauce over, swirling them together gently. Sprinkle the remaining cheese on top.

Cover the dish with foil, creating a dome shape to prevent the foil from sticking to the cheese. Bake in the preheated oven for 45 minutes, then remove the foil and finish under the grill (broiler) for 5 minutes, or until the cheese bubbles and turns golden brown. Let it rest briefly before serving.

SERVES 5

This recipe came about because of my husband. He loves a good sandwich, always has, and this quickly became his favourite. This was one of those recipes I posted online and didn't think much of until it became my most viewed recipe, and easily my most popular during Ramadan. Buy thinly sliced steak from a Somali butcher – they use a deli slicer to get these paper-thin steaks – if you can, or just make sure whatever steak you use is shaved as thinly as possible.

Cheesesteak Sandwiches

2 tbsp olive oil
1 white onion, finely chopped
5–6 slices Somali steak or very thinly sliced steak (200–250 g/7–9 oz)
1 tbsp meat/steak seasoning
1 tbsp smoked paprika
1 tsp ground cumin
1 tsp garlic powder
⅓ tsp black pepper
salt, to taste
1 green (bell) pepper, finely chopped
15 g/½ oz/1 tbsp unsalted butter
5 brioche hotdog rolls
45 g/1½ oz/½ cup grated Cheddar

For the cheese sauce
5 burger cheese squares
2–3 tbsp milk (any milk will work)

For the garlic butter
15 g/½ oz/1 tbsp unsalted butter
1 tsp garlic purée
1 tbsp chopped coriander (cilantro) or parsley
pinch of salt

Equipment
28 x 16-cm/11 x 6½-inch baking dish, lightly greased

Start by heating the oil in a frying pan (skillet) over medium heat. Add the onion and cook for a few minutes until softened. Add the sliced steak, along with the meat seasoning, paprika, cumin, garlic powder and black pepper. Stir well and cook for about 2 minutes. Add salt to taste, then add the green pepper and butter, cooking for an additional 3–5 minutes until the meat is tender. Remove from the heat and set aside.

Preheat the oven to 180°C fan/200°C/400°F/gas mark 6.

Slice the brioche rolls in half and place the bottom halves in the prepared baking dish, leaving the tops aside for now.

Make the cheese sauce. In a microwave-safe bowl, tear the cheese slices into smaller pieces and add 2 tablespoons of the milk. Microwave in 30-second intervals, stirring well each time, until the cheese is melted and smooth. If the mixture is too thick, add an extra tablespoon of milk.

Spoon about three-quarters of the cheese sauce over the bases of the rolls, then top with the cooked steak mixture and sprinkle over the grated Cheddar. Drizzle an extra tablespoon of cheese sauce over the top, then place the tops of the rolls back on.

For the garlic butter, melt the butter in a small bowl and stir in the garlic purée, chopped coriander or parsley and a pinch of salt.

Brush the garlic butter over the tops of the rolls. Cover the dish with foil and bake in the preheated oven for 10–12 minutes.

Serve warm with the remaining cheese sauce on the side.

MAKES 12

I'm an aunt many times over, yes 12 times over (mashaAllah), and these cheeseburger sliders have become a go-to whenever the kids come over. I've made them so many times, I've lost count. Soft buns, melted cheese and seasoned beef – there's never any left. They're easy to prepare ahead of time and they reheat well, which makes them perfect for Ramadan, especially when you're feeding a big family like mine or hosting. I usually bake a big tray and let everyone pull them apart at the table. It's simple, familiar and always a crowd-pleaser.

Cheeseburger Sliders

350 g/12 oz minced (ground) beef
1 tbsp breadcrumbs
1 tsp meat seasoning
1 tsp Vegeta or all-purpose seasoning
¼ tsp black pepper
½ tsp salt (optional)
12 mini brioche rolls
1 tsp ground oregano
1 tsp English mustard
2 tbsp mayonnaise
90 g/3 oz/1 cup grated cheese (I use Red Leicester)
2 tbsp grated Parmesan
12 pickle or gherkin slices
6 slices Gouda (substitute with what you like)
melted butter, for brushing
sesame seeds, for sprinkling

Optional additions

grilled mushrooms, onions or peppers

Equipment

baking sheet, lined with foil

Start by heating a frying pan over medium heat. Add the beef, breadcrumbs, your preferred meat seasoning, Vegeta seasoning, black pepper and salt, if using. Cook, breaking up the mince, until the meat is fully browned, but not cooked through. Remove from the heat and set aside.

Preheat the oven to 180°C fan/200°C/400°F/gas mark 6.

Slice the mini brioche rolls in half and place the bottom halves on the prepared baking sheet, leaving the tops aside for now.

Transfer the browned beef to a bowl. Add the oregano, mustard, mayonnaise, grated cheese and Parmesan. Mix everything together, but be careful not to overmix or you will risk drying it out too much.

Spoon the beef mixture onto the bottom buns, pressing it down slightly. Top each with a sliced pickle, and if desired, add grilled mushrooms, onions or peppers. Lay the Gouda slices on top of the meat mixture, then place the bun lids on top. Brush the tops with melted butter and sprinkle with sesame seeds.

Cover the bread with foil and bake in the preheated oven for 25 minutes, turning the tray around halfway through to ensure even cooking.

Sheet Pan Pizza

SERVES 6-8

This is the pizza I always make at home. The dough has crisp edges and is more light and airy than chewy. Some might say it leans more towards focaccia than pizza – and maybe it does – but let's agree it sits somewhere in-between. You can make the dough up to two days ahead and keep it in the fridge, which makes it easy to prepare when you need it. I usually top mine with pepperoni and a drizzle of hot honey, but feel free to play around with the toppings.

500 g/1 lb 2 oz/generous 3½ cups strong white bread flour, plus an extra 2 tbsp
1 tsp salt
5 g/½ tbsp fast-action yeast
1 tbsp olive oil, plus extra for greasing and drizzling

For the sauce
½ x 400-g/14-oz can chopped tomatoes
1 tsp maple syrup or granulated sugar
1 tbsp tomato purée (paste)
½ tsp salt

For the topping
300 g/10½ oz/3¼ cups pre-grated mozzarella
340 g/12 oz pepperoni slices
honey, for drizzling (optional)

Equipment
23 x 30-cm/9 x 12-inch baking tray

In a large mixing bowl, combine the bread flour, salt, yeast and 390 ml/1⅔ cups of room temperature water, mixing well to form a sticky dough. Add the additional 2 tablespoons of flour and mix again until the dough is sticky but forms a ball. Drizzle the olive oil over the top, spreading it evenly. Cover with a kitchen towel and let the dough rest for 30 minutes.

After 30 minutes, uncover and pull the edges of the dough toward the centre, working around the full circle. Repeat this one more time, then cover and let rest for another 30 minutes.

Repeat the folding step one more time, noticing the added elasticity. Very lightly oil a large container and transfer the dough into it, adding a light drizzle of olive oil on top. Cover directly with clingfilm (plastic wrap), seal with a lid and refrigerate overnight.

When ready to make the pizza, oil a baking tray with sides (sheet pan) and turn the dough out onto it. Let it rest for 20–30 minutes.

Meanwhile, preheat the oven to 230°C fan/250°C/500°F/gas mark 9).

For the sauce, add the tomatoes, syrup or sugar, tomato purée and salt to a small saucepan over medium heat. Cook for about 5 minutes, then adjust salt to taste and remove from the heat.

Stretch the dough to the edges of the sheet pan. Spread the tomato sauce across it evenly, covering the entire surface. Top with the mozzarella, followed by the pepperoni slices.

Place the sheet pan on the lower shelf of the oven and bake for about 20 minutes, or until golden brown. Drizzle with honey, if desired, slice and serve warm.

SERVES 4

Chicken shawarma is one of the most iconic and addictive street foods across the Middle East. If I'm there, you'll find me at a shawarma stand almost daily. Nothing else compares. That said, this version comes surprisingly close, and it's the charcoal smoking at the end that gives it that unmistakable spit-roast flavour. You can serve it wrapped in flatbread with toum and pickles, then lightly toast the whole thing, or bring it all to the table and let everyone build their own. Either way, expect people to ask for the recipe or quietly hope you make it again.

Chicken Shawarma

2 tbsp olive oil, plus ½ tsp for drizzling
2 tbsp distilled vinegar
2 tbsp tomato purée (paste)
2 tsp crushed garlic
1 tsp ground turmeric
1 tsp ground cumin
1 tsp ground coriander
1 tsp ground allspice
2 tsp smoked paprika
½ tsp cayenne pepper
1¼ tsp salt
1 tsp granulated sugar
700–800 g/1 lb 9 oz–1 lb 12 oz skinless and boneless chicken thighs
6–8 small round pitas
sliced baby pickles, to serve

For the toum
65 g/½ cup garlic cloves
1 tsp kosher salt, or ½ tsp salt
350 ml/1½ cups sunflower oil, or any colourless oil
about 3 tbsp lemon juice

Equipment
1 small briquette instant-lighting coal

In a bowl, combine the olive oil, vinegar, tomato purée, garlic, turmeric, cumin, coriander, allspice, smoked paprika, cayenne, salt and sugar. Mix thoroughly to form a smooth paste. Wash and clean the chicken, then coat it evenly with the seasoning mixture. Cover and refrigerate for a few hours to marinate.

When ready to cook, preheat the oven to 180°C fan/200°C/400°F/gas mark 6.

Heat a cast-iron pan over medium–high heat. Once hot, add the chicken, cooking it in batches to avoid overcrowding, and ensuring the pan stays hot and the chicken sears instead of sautéing. Cook each batch for 3–4 minutes per side until golden and slightly charred. Transfer the chicken to a baking dish and bake in the oven for 15 minutes to finish cooking through.

While the chicken cooks, prepare the toum. In a blender, blend the garlic and salt until minced. With the blender running, very slowly begin to drizzle in the oil through the small opening in the lid. Once you have added half the oil, begin to alternate between adding the remaining oil and the lemon juice, adding it a tablespoon at a time. If your blender struggles, add 2–3 tablespoons of cold water to help it blend smoothly. Transfer to a bowl and set aside.

Once the chicken is cooked, remove it from the oven. Place a piece of coal on a small piece of foil alongside the chicken in the oven dish, then light the coal. Quickly drizzle ½ teaspoon of oil over the coal to create smoke, then immediately cover the dish tightly with foil or a tight-fitting lid to trap the smoke. Let it sit for 2 minutes to infuse a smoky flavour.

Transfer the chicken to a chopping board and slice it into small pieces to replicate shawarma.

Heat the cast-iron pan over medium heat again. Lightly dab each pitta into the chicken juices left in the oven dish, ensuring an even coating without soaking. Briefly heat the pitta on both sides in the cast-iron pan.

To assemble, spread a layer of toum on the flavoured side of each pitta, add some chicken, and top with sliced pickles. Roll tightly, then optionally heat the roll in the pan to help it hold its shape. Serve immediately or individually wrap in foil to enjoy later.

SERVES 4

This is another homage to my Egyptian heritage. Made with layers of aubergine, tomatoes and garlic, it's a dish that's all about simple ingredients coming together. It can be served warm or cold, on the side or right in the middle of the table. However it's served, I think it always finds its place.

Mesa'a'ah *Aubergine and Tomato Stew*

2 large aubergines (eggplants), sliced into 2-cm/¾-inch thick rounds, then quartered
¼ tsp salt, plus extra for salting the aubergines
250 ml/1 cup olive oil, plus extra if needed
1 onion, thinly sliced
4–6 garlic cloves, thinly sliced
1 tbsp tomato purée (paste)
1½ tsp ground cumin
1 tsp ground coriander
½ tsp paprika
1 tsp honey
500 g/1 lb 2 oz ripe tomatoes, roughly chopped
juice of ½ lemon
4 tbsp finely chopped parsley

Sprinkle the aubergine slices generously with salt and place them in a colander for 45 minutes–1 hour. This helps draw out excess moisture and bitterness.

In a large deep frying pan (skillet), heat the olive oil over medium heat until it reaches 180°C/350°F, or until a cube of bread browns in 30 seconds. Fry the aubergine slices in batches for 2–3 minutes per side, or until golden brown. Be careful not to overcrowd the pan, as this can prevent even cooking. Once the aubergines are golden, remove them from the oil and place them on paper towels to drain. If there's any excess oil left in the pan, carefully pour out most of it, leaving only 1 tablespoon in the pan for the sauce.

To the same pan, add the onion and cook over medium heat for about 5 minutes, stirring occasionally, until softened. Add the garlic and continue cooking for another 2–3 minutes until fragrant.

Lower the heat slightly, stir in the tomato purée and cook for 4–5 minutes. The paste should darken slightly, the oil will separate, and it may stick slightly to the pan. This is normal and enhances flavour.

Stir in the salt, cumin, coriander, paprika and honey, ensuring the spices are evenly distributed. Add the chopped tomatoes and mix well. Lower the heat and cook for 8–10 minutes, stirring occasionally, until the tomatoes break down and the sauce thickens to a rich consistency. If the sauce is too thick, add 1–2 tablespoons of water.

Once the sauce is ready, gently add the fried aubergine slices to the pan. Use a spoon to coat the aubergine lightly in the sauce, being careful not to break the slices. Lower the heat to a simmer and cook for 15–20 minutes to allow the flavours to meld.

Turn off the heat, squeeze the lemon juice over the dish, and garnish with freshly chopped parsley. This dish is best served at room temperature or refrigerated and served cold.

BREADS

Bread has become something I've grown into. As I've gotten older and more confident in the kitchen, I've found myself turning to it more and more. There's something calming about it, something grounding. It requires time and a bit of care, but never rushes you. It asks for your hands, your patience, and in return, it gives back so much comfort.

Some breads, like *laxoox* (see page 117), are stitched into my earliest memories. My mum made it every weekend without fail. I'd smother mine with butter and sugar, then pour tea right over the top, a tradition that might sound unusual, but is pure Somali nostalgia. That buttery, sweet mess was always the best part of my morning. *Kimis* (see page 123) is another one that's always been there. My mum made it growing up, and now that I'm married, my mother-in-law brings it over every weekend. It's soft, warm and layered with love. Something passed between generations, now made for us and her granddaughter too.

And now, I make bread with my daughter. It's become our quiet ritual. She knows the rhythm, the feel of the dough, the pride that comes with pulling something golden from the oven. It's even become something people know her for, 'the one who makes bread.' I love that. I love that she's growing up with it the way I did, hands in flour, surrounded by warmth.

There are other breads I reach for throughout the year, soft dinner rolls (see page 131) or folded *malawax* (see page 120) – each one serving a purpose, each one easy to love. Bread has a way of bringing people to the table. You don't need to explain it. Just tear, dip, wrap and eat.

Then there are the ones that only come around during Ramadan including, of course, samosa sheets (see page 126). Making them is a ritual in itself. In the days leading up to Ramadan, we gather as a family and spend hours preparing. Most families do. Everyone has a role: someone mixing the filling, someone folding, someone sealing. It's repetitive, a little tiring, but there's always chatter, laughter and the comfort of doing something together, year after year.

This chapter brings together all the breads that have shaped my kitchen, from the everyday to the celebratory. Some are soft and pillowy, others crisp and delicate. Some carry memory, others tradition, and many now feel like my own. However you make them, I hope they bring warmth to your table and joy to those you share them with.

MAKES 8–10

Laxoox, also known as *canjeero*, is a fermented flatbread that is usually served in the morning. It shares similarities with Ethiopian *injera*, but the taste is gentler, and the texture and size make it more suited to everyday cooking. These are eaten for breakfast or with stews, soft and warm straight from the pan. My favourite way to have them is spread with butter, sprinkled with sugar, and with black tea poured over the top. Just make sure to save a little batter as a starter for the next batch.

Laxoox (Canjeero) *Fermented Pancakes*

200 g/7 oz/1½ cups plain (all-purpose) flour
70 g/2½ oz/½ cup sorghum flour
70 g/2½ oz/½ cup wholemeal (whole-wheat) flour
½ tbsp fast-action dried yeast
2 tbsp sugar, plus extra to serve
1 tsp flaxseed
¼ tsp salt
500 ml/2 cups lukewarm water
sunflower oil, for greasing
ghee or butter, to serve

In a large bowl, combine the plain flour, sorghum flour, wholemeal flour, yeast, sugar, flaxseed and salt. Mix well to ensure everything is evenly distributed.

Gradually pour in 250 ml/1 cup of lukewarm water and mix thoroughly using a handheld mixer. Once incorporated, add the remaining 250 ml/1 cup of water and continue mixing for 3–4 minutes. Turn the bowl as you mix to ensure the batter is smooth and lump-free.

Cover the bowl with a clean kitchen towel or plate and let the batter rest on the counter for 30 minutes–1 hour. The batter should rise slightly and develop small bubbles.

When ready to cook, heat a cast-iron or non-stick pan over medium heat. Add a small drop of oil to the pan and use a folded piece of paper towel to spread and wipe away the excess oil. Keep the paper towel nearby, as you'll use it to re-grease the pan throughout the cooking process.

Before cooking, give the batter a gentle stir with a ladle. The batter should have a bubbly appearance and a light, pourable consistency. If there are no bubbles, allow the batter to rest for an additional 10–20 minutes.

Continued overleaf

Once the pan is hot, ladle about 175 ml/¾ cup of batter into the centre. Using the back of the ladle, gently spread the batter in a circular motion from the centre outward to create an even layer, about 2–3 mm/⅛ inch thick. You should see bubbles forming immediately – this is key to the texture of laxoox. Cover the pan with a lid and cook for 2–3 minutes. The batter should set, and the surface will appear dry, spongy and slightly golden at the edges. Do not flip the laxoox.

Remove and transfer the laxoox to a plate. Repeat the process, ensuring the pan is lightly greased between each one. Optionally, spread the laxoox with ghee or butter and sprinkle with sugar before serving with tea.

Tips: Traditionally, *laxoox* pairs well with dishes like *suqaar* (see page 84) or *fuul* (see page 63), making it a versatile addition to Somali meals.

To make a starter for the next batch, reserve 125 ml/½ cup of the batter and transfer it to a clean airtight container. Leave it at room temperature for the rest of the day, then refrigerate it. For the next batch, omit the yeast and mix this reserved batter into the new mixture. This acts as a continuous starter and enhances the flavour and texture over time. Repeat this process with every subsequent batch. The starter will keep up to 2 months without feeding.

MAKES 10

This is a traditional Somali flatbread with a slightly dense but soft texture and a golden crust. It's traditionally baked in a clay oven, but at home I make it in a skillet, hence the name *muufo taawa*. You can easily use a regular frying pan too. It's a staple in many Somali homes, especially in the south, and reminds me a little of a thick pitta. I grew up seeing it paired with *suugo* (see page 97) or *suqaar* (see page 84), or just torn and dipped into whatever was on the table. It's simple and quietly nostalgic.

Muufo *Flatbread*

280 g/10 oz/2 cups strong bread flour
350 g/12 oz/2½ cups plain (all-purpose) flour, plus extra for dusting
1 tbsp fast-action dried yeast
1 tbsp granulated sugar
1 tsp salt
315 ml/1⅓ cups lukewarm water
2 tbsp Greek yogurt
90 ml/⅓ cup olive oil, plus extra for greasing, drizzling and frying

In a large mixing bowl, combine the bread flour and plain flour, mixing well to ensure they are evenly distributed. Add the yeast, sugar and salt, then stir to combine. Gradually pour in the lukewarm water while mixing, until the dough comes together. Add the Greek yogurt and olive oil and begin to start kneading.

Transfer the dough to a floured surface and continue kneading until it forms a smooth, sticky dough that no longer clings to your hands.

Lightly oil your mixing bowl and place the dough inside, drizzling a tablespoon of olive oil over the top. Cover the bowl with a clean kitchen towel and let the dough rise in a warm place for at least an hour, or until it has doubled in size.

Once risen, turn the dough out onto a generously floured surface and fold it over itself a few times to develop its texture. Pull off small pieces of dough to form 10 balls. One at a time, shape each ball into a circle about 5 mm/¼ inch thick and about 19 cm/7½ inches diameter (this will give it a soft texture).

Place a frying pan (skillet) over high heat, adding a light layer of oil to the surface. Place a circle of dough into the pan, flattening gently if needed. Drizzle a little oil over the top. When bubbles begin to form, usually in about 30 seconds, flip and cook the other side until golden.

Remove and keep the cooked bread under a kitchen towel to maintain softness while you cook the rest.

MAKES 5–6

Malawax was always made at the weekend, and it was always made for Ramadan. My mum would stack them high and somehow keep them warm until breakfast was ready. I try to carry on the same habit now for my daughter, and during Ramadan too. They're soft, slightly sweet, and similar to a crêpe, but what makes them different is the butter that's spread on top just before flipping. It gives them those deep, dark blisters that we all love. The more blisters, the better. One of my mum's tips, only for Ramadan, was to cut them into eighths, pour over melted butter mixed with sugar, and seal them until iftar. It keeps them soft and stops you from eating four without realising.

Malawax (Malawah) *Sweet Crêpes*

140 g/5 oz/1 cup plus 1 tbsp plain (all-purpose) flour
1 egg
1 tsp ground cinnamon (optional)
175 ml/¾ cup milk, warmed (any milk will work)
60 ml/¼ cup warm water, plus extra if needed
sunflower oil, for frying
30 g/1 oz/2 tbsp butter, melted
1 tbsp granulated sugar

Begin by adding the flour, egg, cinnamon (if using) and milk to a blender and blend until smooth. Gradually pour in the warm water, stirring until you achieve a loose, smooth consistency. If the batter is too thick, add a little extra warm water to thin it out.

Heat a frying pan over medium heat. Lightly coat the pan with a small amount of oil, then wipe away any excess using a folded paper towel. Keep the paper nearby for reuse if you need more oil later. Once the pan is hot, use one hand to pour a ladleful of the batter into the pan, and the other to swirl the pan around to coat the bottom of the pan evenly with the batter. Cook for 30–40 seconds until the malawax is 70–80 per cent cooked – at this point you will notice the colour of the batter changing – then drizzle a teaspoon of melted butter over the surface and flip it over. Gently press down with a spatula to ensure even browning.

Once cooked – it should be golden with brown spots on the surface – transfer to a plate and sprinkle some of the sugar on it. Repeat with the remaining batter and sugar.

MAKES 10

Kimis, also known as *sabaayad*, is a popular unleavened flatbread with deep cultural significance, particularly during Ramadan throughout East and North Africa. Made from a simple dough that is rolled into layers, this classic bread has a flaky, slightly crispy texture. It's incredibly versatile, complementing hearty stews like *suqaar* (see page 84), or served with sweet honey, or simply sprinkled with sugar and dipped into a cup of tea (my personal favourite!).

Kimis (Sabaayad) *Flaky Flatbread*

7 tbsp sunflower oil, plus extra for frying
560 g/1 lb 4 oz/4¼ cups plain (all-purpose) flour, plus extra for dusting
pinch of salt
225 ml/scant 1 cup warm water

Add 2 tablespoons of the oil to a small saucepan and place over medium-high heat.

In a large bowl, combine the flour and salt. Create a well in the centre and pour in the hot oil. Let it cool slightly, then mix until the dough has a grainy, sand-like texture. Gradually add the warm water, kneading into a soft dough. Shape into a large ball, rub with a little oil, cover and let it rest for at least 1 hour.

Turn the dough out onto a lightly floured surface, where it should feel noticeably softer. If the dough feels too elastic, let it rest a few minutes more. Knead briefly and divide it into 10 equal pieces. Roll out a portion to the size of a small dinner plate. Lightly dust the surface with flour.

Roll it out until 5 mm/¼ inch thick and about 19 cm/7½ inches square. Brush with ½ tablespoon of oil. Fold one side of the dough towards the centre, then repeat on the other side to form a neat rectangle. Grab both ends, gently stretch, and smack it slightly on the counter to elongate the dough. Fold it over itself from one side to the other to form a small, layered square.

Repeat with each piece, brushing with ½ tablespoon of oil and dusting with flour before rolling out. Keep the rolled pieces covered as you work to avoid them drying out. Once you have made all 10, gently roll each piece again into a square or circle about 5 mm/¼ inch thick, being careful not to press too hard to maintain the layers. This method ensures the kimis will be soft and flaky.

Heat a tablespoon of oil in a large cast-iron frying pan (skillet) over medium heat. Place one of the kimis into the hot pan and cook for 1-2 minutes, moving it around in the pan, until a light golden colour and puffing in some spots. Lightly drizzle with oil, then turn over and lightly brush the cooked side with oil. Cook for another 1-2 minutes, then flip one last time, brush with oil, and cook for an additional 30 seconds-1 minute. While each kimis cooks, roll out the next.

Transfer the cooked kimis to a clean kitchen towel, fold it in half, then fold over again into a triangle. This folding method will ensure the bread softens. Cover with the towel to keep the cooked kimis soft and flaky as you cook the rest.

BREADS

MAKES 36

It's pretty much agreed across most Muslim communities that *sambuus*, also known as samosas, will be on the table during Ramadan. A few weeks before the holy month, friends and family gather around the table to fold *sambuus*. This quiet tradition involves stacks of wrappers, bowls of filling and hours of conversation. It's one of those rituals that signals Ramadan is near, long before the first date is eaten. There's always laughter, someone perfecting their folding technique, and trays slowly filling up with rows of sambuus ready for the freezer.

You can find multiple variations of *sambuus* across different regions and cultures but in my opinion hands down Somali *sambuus* triumphs. The combination of the crispy pastry and the filling is divine. If you haven't tried a tuna *sambuus* (see page 48), this is your sign. It's the best filling and you honestly can't tell me otherwise.

Sambuus (Samosa) Sheets *Fooliyo (Warqadda) Sambuusaha*

350 g/12 oz/2½ cups plain (all-purpose) flour, plus extra for dusting
½ tsp salt
225 ml/8fl oz/1 cup warm water
sunflower oil, for brushing

In a large mixing bowl, combine the flour and salt. Gradually pour in the warm water, stirring until a sticky dough forms. The dough should feel slightly tacky but should not stick to your hands when touched. Divide the dough into nine equal-sized balls. Cover the dough balls with a kitchen towel and allow them to rest for 5 minutes.

Lightly flour your work surface. Take three dough balls and roll them out to about 10 cm/4 inches diameter. Brush one rolled sheet with a thin layer of oil, then sprinkle lightly with flour. Place a second sheet on top, repeating the oil and flour process. Add the third sheet, pressing down gently to secure the layers. Lightly dust the top with flour.

Using a rolling pin, roll out the stacked sheets into a larger circle, about 20 cm/8 inches diameter. As you roll, gently hold one side of the dough with one hand while rolling with the other to prevent the layers from separating. If the layers begin to pull apart, carefully stretch them back into place. While perfection is not essential, aim to keep the layers as close as possible around the edges. Once rolled to the desired size, cut the dough into quarters, creating four triangular pieces.

Repeat with the remaining six balls of dough, working with three at a time. You should have 12 triangles.

Heat a frying pan (skillet) over high heat, then reduce the heat to medium-low. Place one of the dough triangles onto the skillet. Cook just until the dough changes colour, avoiding any browning. Flip and cook the other side briefly. Remove from the pan and place under a clean kitchen towel to keep warm. Repeat this process with the remaining dough triangles.

Once all the triangles have been cooked, carefully peel back the individual layers from each triangle. You should end up with approximately 36 thin sheets, though this may vary if any layers tear. For a more uniform appearance (though not necessary), you can trim the edges of the sheets to create neat, even triangles.

Tip: The sheets can be stored in the freezer, wrapped in a freezer bag. Ensure they're pulled apart before freezing.

BREADS 129

MAKES 12–16

If there's one thing I'm always expected to show up with, it's these dinner rolls. Whether it's iftar, a family gathering or just an excuse to share a meal, this is what I bring. They're unbelievably soft and pillowy, and the garlic butter on top takes them somewhere special. They're also incredibly forgiving. I've made them with wholemeal (wholewheat) flour, added cheese, thrown in seeds and even used them as burger or hotdog buns. Whatever I do, they still work. With any luck, these will be the softest, most reliable rolls you'll ever bake.

Dinner Rolls

250 ml/1 cup milk, warmed
2 tbsp granulated sugar
1 tbsp fast-action dried yeast
1 egg
50 g/1¾ oz/3½ tbsp unsalted butter, softened, plus 3 tbsp melted butter, for brushing
1 tsp salt
400 g/14 oz/3 cups plain (all-purpose) flour, plus extra for dusting and if needed

For the garlic butter
2 tbsp unsalted butter, melted
3 garlic cloves, minced
1 tbsp fresh parsley, finely chopped
flaky sea salt, to finish

Equipment
23 x 30-cm/9 x 12-inch baking tray, lightly oiled

In a large mixing bowl, whisk together the warm milk, sugar and yeast until the mixture begins to froth slightly. Leave it to rest for 5 minutes to activate the yeast.

Add the egg to the mixture and mix until combined. Stir in the softened butter and salt, followed by half of the flour, and mix until incorporated. Add the remaining flour and mix until a rough dough forms. If the dough feels too wet to knead, add a tablespoon of flour at a time, mixing gently, until the dough comes together. It should be soft and slightly sticky, but manageable. Be careful not to over-add flour, as this can result in a dense dough.

Turn the dough onto a lightly floured surface and knead by hand until it becomes smooth and elastic. To test if it's ready, gently poke the dough; if it slowly bounces back, it's ready to rise.

Lightly oil the dough and place it in a clean mixing bowl. Cover and let it rise in a warm place until doubled in size. Once risen, gently press the air out of the dough in the bowl. Fold the dough on itself a few times to create layers, then carefully shape it back into a ball without additional kneading.

Divide the dough into 12–16 equal pieces. Slightly flatten each piece, folding and pinching underneath to form a smooth ball, then roll gently in your palm to finish shaping. Arrange the dough balls on the greased baking tray. Cover and leave to rise again for 30 minutes.

Preheat the oven to 180°C fan/200°C/400°F/gas mark 6.

Brush the tops of the rolls with some melted butter and place them in the oven. Bake for 20–25 minutes, or until golden brown, rotating the tray halfway through, if needed, for even colouring.

While the rolls bake, combine the melted butter, garlic and parsley in a small bowl. When the rolls come out of the oven, brush them generously with the garlic butter and sprinkle with flaky sea salt. Serve warm.

MAKES 20–25

In Somali, *bur* simply means 'flour', but it's also the name for this style of fried dough, similar to *mandazi*, but with its own feel. These are light and hollow, crisp on the outside and light and fluffy inside. The key is spooning hot oil over the dough as it fries – that is what creates the pocket of air. As for the shape, that's entirely up to you. Triangles, circles, diamonds, whatever feels right – just make sure to stuff dates inside before eating!

Bur *Cardamom-Spiced Beignets*

3 tbsp granulated sugar
3 tbsp sunflower oil, plus extra for greasing and frying
1 tbsp fast-action dried yeast
225 ml/scant 1 cup milk, warmed
350 g/12 oz/⅔ cups plain (all-purpose) flour, plus extra if needed and for dusting
¼ tsp ground cardamom (optional)
icing (confectioners') sugar, for dusting (optional)

Start by adding the sugar, oil and yeast to a large bowl. Pour in most of the warm milk, reserving 2–3 tablespoons for later use. Whisk the mixture together until the yeast has completely dissolved.

Stir the flour into the mixture until well combined. If using, add the cardamom at this stage. If the dough feels too dry after mixing, add the reserved milk; if it's too wet, mix in an extra 1–2 tablespoons of flour. Knead the dough thoroughly until smooth, then form it into a large ball.

Place the dough in an oiled bowl to prevent sticking, cover and set it in a warm, dark place to prove for at least 30 minutes. You can leave it longer, but don't leave it too long, as this can risk an overly yeasty flavour.

Once the dough has risen, roll it out on a well-floured surface and fold it over a few times. Divide the dough into five balls, then roll each ball out individually to a 15-cm/6-inch circle, about 5 mm/¼ inch thick. Cut each circle into four to five triangles, or any shape you prefer. I often use a cup to cut out circles. After cutting, dust both sides with flour.

Heat sunflower oil in a pan until it reaches 180°C/350°F, or until a cube of bread browns in 30 seconds, and carefully add the dough pieces, working in batches to avoid overcrowding the pan and ensuring the oil isn't too hot, as it can cook the exterior quicker than the inside. Cook until the dough shapes rise to the top and puff up. Gently pour hot oil over them using a spoon to help them puff up more. Once golden brown on one side, flip them over and fry briefly on the other side before removing with a slotted spoon (the second side doesn't need as long to cook).

Drain on paper towels and leave to cool, then enjoy them as they are or dust with icing sugar for a sweet treat.

SPICES & CHUTNEYS

Behind every dish in this cookbook is something small that makes a big difference: a spoon of *xawaash* (see page 142) in the rice; a drizzle of *bisbaas* over meat; a swipe of *shidni* (see page 138) on the side of a plate. These might seem like extras, but in Somali cooking, they're the heartbeat. And while this book carries dishes from across different countries and cultures, my heritage is Somali and these are the flavours that represent Ramadan to me. They bring fire, depth, brightness and balance. They stretch beyond Somali food, blending beautifully with whatever they're paired with. These are the quiet heroes that carry so much of the flavour. They add small additions that change everything. And they're delicious and always the first thing people ask about when the plate is cleared.

Growing up, there was always a jar of something spicy in the fridge. *Shidni*, thick with tomatoes and heat. *Bisbaas qumbe* (see page 139), sharp and full of coconut, a staple on the side of rice dishes. Or *bisbaas cagaar* (see page 141), green and punchy and so fresh it wakes everything up. *Xawaash*, the signature Somali spice blend, lived in an unlabelled jar that never seemed to run out. These weren't made every day, but they were always there ready to be stirred in or spooned over.

During Ramadan, these additions become even more important. After a day of fasting, they're what make that first plate feel alive. Whether it's the zing of *bisbaas* over *sambuus* (see page 48), or the way *xawaash* lingers in a slow-cooked stew, these are the things that quietly tie everything together.

This chapter is a celebration of those small things that carry big memories. They come from my Somali kitchen, shaped by the way I cook now. I hope they find a permanent place in your fridge, and on your table too.

MAKES 1 MEDIUM JAR

Often used as a dip or accompaniment, *shidni* is made by sautéing a blend of spices with fresh ingredients to create a rich, flavourful sauce. There are countless variations of this chutney, each with unique ingredients and preparation methods. This version combines dates and tamarind for a perfect balance of sweetness and acidity. While I rely on premade tamarind paste in my kitchen, in Somalia, tamarind pods are soaked in water and then squeezed to produce a thick, tangy paste. I remember, as a child, mixing the juice with water and sugar for a refreshingly tart drink – though that is a recipe for another time!

Shidni *Sweet and Spicy Chutney*

4 green finger chillies (chiles), tops removed, seeds left in
½ small onion
4–5 garlic cloves
4 Medjool dates, pitted
60 ml/¼ cup sunflower oil
400-g/14-oz can finely chopped tomatoes
2 tsp concentrated tamarind paste
2 tsp Vegeta or all-purpose seasoning
2 tsp granulated sugar

Begin by blending the green chillies, onion, garlic and dates in a blender until smooth. (If the dates are firm, soak them in boiling water for 30 minutes to soften, reserving the soaking water for later.)

Heat the oil in a saucepan over medium heat. Once hot, add the blended mixture, the chopped tomatoes, tamarind paste, seasoning, sugar and 125 ml/½ cup of water. If the dates were soaked, use the reserved soaking water in place of the water. Stir well to combine.

Cover and simmer on medium–low heat for 1 hour, stirring occasionally, until the oil rises to the surface. Once cooled, transfer to an airtight container and store in the fridge for up to 4 weeks.

Tip: If you can't find finely chopped tomatoes, just blitz regular chopped tomatoes in the blender until they reach a fine consistency.

MAKES 2 MEDIUM JARS

Somali cuisine is known for its aromatic spices, such as cumin and cardamom, but it's not typically known for being overly spicy. That said, the heat often comes from *bisbaas*, a popular hot sauce served alongside meals for those, like me, who enjoy a little extra kick. Made with fresh coconut, green chillies, and a blend of spices, it has a smoother, milder heat compared to the tangier, sharper varieties found elsewhere in this book and the country. My secret ingredient? Mayonnaise – recommended by a good friend of mine. It brings a rich, velvety creaminess that softens the fiery heat and tangy kick from the green chillies, creating a perfect balance of flavours in the chutney.

Bisbaas Qumbe *Coconut Chilli Sauce*

8 finger chillies (chiles), tops removed, seeds left in
1 shallot, peeled and cut in half
130g/4½ oz/½ cup plain yogurt
1 tsp salt
40 g/1½ oz/½ cup desiccated (dried unsweetened shredded) coconut
1 lemon, peeled
3–4 garlic cloves
2 tbsp mayonnaise
1 tsp granulated sugar

Begin by adding the chillies, shallot, yogurt, salt, desiccated coconut and peeled lemon into a blender. Blend until smooth. Add the garlic and blend again until fully incorporated.

Transfer the mixture to a bowl and stir in the mayonnaise and sugar until well combined. Taste and adjust the salt as needed.

Store in an airtight container in the fridge for up to 3 weeks.

MAKES 1 MEDIUM JAR

Somali food isn't known for being fiery, but that's only because the heat lives in the sauce. *Bisbaas* is one of those condiments that brings the whole plate to life. If you've ever been to a Somali restaurant and spotted a little green sauce on the side, you've probably noticed how quickly it grabs everyone's attention. It's not your usual chilli sauce. It's sweet, tangy, spicy and sharp all at once. The sweetness comes from dates, the tang from tamarind and the heat from fresh green chillies. This is the version I come back to every time, especially during Ramadan. Even in homes where it's not made often, it somehow always appears during the holy month. You can easily adjust the heat. If you prefer something hotter, add more chillies and cut back on the dates, and the result will be a brighter, greener version.

Bisbaas Cagaar *Somali Chilli Sauce*

10 green finger chillies (chiles), tops removed, seeds left in
1 tomato
3 Medjool dates, pitted
6 garlic cloves
½ tsp tamarind paste
⅓ tsp salt, or to taste
squeeze of lemon juice

In a blender, combine the green chillies, tomato, dates, garlic, tamarind paste, salt and 50 ml/3½ tablespoons of water. Blend until completely smooth. Taste and adjust the salt as needed.

Pour into an airtight jar and store in the refrigerator for up to 4 weeks. When ready to serve, add a squeeze of fresh lemon juice; adding it earlier will cause bitterness in the sauce.

MAKES 1 SMALL JAR

The word 'xawaash' means 'spice'. While it can refer to any individual spice or blend, in this context it describes a savoury mix used to season meats, rice, stews and just about everything in-between.

If you're cooking from this book, you'll come across it often. It's the backbone of so many of the dishes I make, especially during Ramadan, when the cooking feels a little more intentional, a little more rooted. Every household has their own version. This version leans more heavily on cumin and skips the clove (which is commonly used, but I've always found it overwhelms the rest). This version is balanced, earthy and just warm enough. The spices that make *xawaash* aren't unique to Somalia. They're ever-present across the regions explored in this book, forming the foundation of dishes from East Africa to the Arabian Peninsula. It's a reminder of how connected our kitchens really are. Once you've made a jar and tucked it into your cupboard, you'll find yourself reaching for it constantly.

Xawaash (Hawaash) *Somali Spice Mix*

30 g/1 oz/6 tbsp coriander seeds
30 g/1 oz/4½ tbsp cumin seeds
36–40 cardamom pods
2 tbsp ground cinnamon, (freshly ground is preferable, see Tip)
½ tsp black peppercorns
1 tsp ground turmeric

Begin by adding the coriander and cumin seeds to a pan over medium heat. Stir continuously until they're lightly toasted and aromatic, then remove from the heat and let them cool.

Place the cooled spices into a grinder along with the cardamom, cinnamon and peppercorns (leave out the turmeric for now). Grind to a fine powder, then sift through a fine sieve (strainer) into a bowl. Return any coarse bits in the sieve to the grinder and process again until smooth.

Stir in the turmeric and transfer the finished spice blend to an airtight container for storage. It will keep for up to 6 months.

Tip: Freshly ground cinnamon works best here; to make your own, grind cinnamon sticks to a fine powder in the blender and take out 2 tbsp for this recipe.

Ramadan isn't really about dessert, but somehow, there's always room for something sweet. Not every night, not every table, but every now and then, a tray appears, quietly anticipated and gratefully received. These are the kinds of desserts that feel gentle, never overindulgent, just enough to round off a meal, to bring a little joy to the end of the evening.

Some of the recipes in this chapter hold deep personal memories. *Kunafa* (see page 161) takes me straight back to a quieter Dubai, long before the city became what it is today. I remember eating it in one particular café all the time, the scent of orange blossom and ghee lingering in the air, the slow pace of it all. Those moments were simple, and so the recipe is also simple. It doesn't need to be complicated to be beautiful.

Others, like my Somali chai tres leches (see page 149), are more recent additions. It's become one of my most popular desserts online. A soft sponge soaked in spiced milk, a cross between tradition and comfort. Then there are the classics like *basbousa* (see page 155), rich with semolina and syrup, and timir cake (see page 152), soft and naturally sweet with dates. These recipes aren't about feasting. They are made to fit into the rhythm of Ramadan. They are not always served but they are always welcomed when they do appear. They are easy to make, made with ingredients you most likely already have, and designed to be shared without fuss. A square of cake, a spoonful of custard, a bite of something warm and sweet. It really doesn't take much.

This chapter is for those quiet cravings and celebratory evenings, for the desserts passed between hands, placed gently on tables, and enjoyed slowly. However you choose to serve them, I hope these recipes bring softness to your Ramadan and Eid, and just the right touch of sweetness.

SERVES 8-10

This is my take on the classic Latin American dessert, but infused with Somali tea spices like cardamom, cinnamon and clove. That warmth completely transforms the milk mixture, and it's one of those recipes I shared online that really took off. So many people tried it and made it their own – which makes it feel all the more special to me. I usually keep it simple and use store-bought madeira cake, but *doolsho* works beautifully too. It's the kind of dessert you can prep the night before, and just before serving, pour over a little saved milk to freshen it up. Now, it's become the thing people expect from me. The same way you'd expect tea and biscuits at someone's house, my guests expect Somali tres leches. And truthfully, I enjoy making it every time.

Somali Chai Tres Leches

150 ml/⅔ cup milk
397-g/14-oz can condensed milk
350 ml/1½ cups evaporated milk
2 tsp Somali tea spice (see page 168)
24 Madeira cake slices (510 g/1 lb 2 oz) or doolsho (see page 209)
500 ml/2 cups double (heavy) or whipping cream
100 g/3½ oz/scant 1 cup icing (confectioners') sugar
1 tsp vanilla bean paste
100 g/3½ oz/1 cup crushed pistachios

Equipment
23 x 30-cm/9 x 12-inch baking dish

Heat the milk, condensed milk and evaporated milk together with the Somali tea spice in a saucepan. Bring it to a gentle simmer, avoiding a boil to prevent the milk from splitting or burning – you just want small bubbles around the edges. Simmer for 5–10 minutes, then strain out the spices and set the milk mixture aside to cool.

Arrange the cake slices in the baking dish, arranging them in two layers if possible. As you lay down each layer, press it down gently to flatten slightly. Use a chopstick to poke holes all over the cake slices, ensuring you reach the bottom of the dish. Reserve 250 ml/1 cup of the milk mixture for serving, then pour the remaining cooled milk mixture over the cake, a little at a time, letting it soak in and settle before adding more.

In a separate bowl, whisk together the cream, icing sugar and vanilla until soft peaks form.

Spread the cream mixture evenly over the cake using a palette knife or metal spatula, then top with the crushed pistachios. Refrigerate for at least 4 hours to allow the cake to set.

When serving, pour a bit of the reserved milk mixture at the base of each slice.

SERVES 6–8

Tiramisu might be Italian, but with the Italian influence in Somalia, it's now a staple in Somali homes. Growing up, my mum made it often, always eggless, because raw eggs? Absolutely not. You couldn't convince her then, and you still can't now. To be fair, it works for more people that way. The funny thing is, I didn't even like tiramisu as a child. Maybe it was the texture, maybe the coffee, I honestly couldn't tell you. And I also couldn't tell you when exactly I fell in love with it. But my mum used to host guests all the time, and she never once served a table without tiramisu. Not once. Now my siblings and I are the same – we all make it, we all love it, and I'm pretty sure most Somalis do too. And if you don't yet… this might be the one that converts you.

Tiramisu

230 ml/scant 1 cup heavy whipping cream, cold
70 g/2½ oz/½ cup icing (confectioners') sugar
230 g/8 oz/1 cup mascarpone
500 ml/2 cups strong coffee, cooled to room temperature
1–2 packs of lady finger biscuits
2 tbsp cocoa powder

Equipment
25 x 18-cm/10 x 7-inch baking dish

Begin by whisking the cream and icing sugar in a mixing bowl until soft peaks form. Once the cream is whipped, add the mascarpone and whisk gently until stiff peaks form, being careful not to overmix as this can turn the mixture into butter.

Put the coffee in a shallow dish for dipping. Quickly dip each lady finger into the coffee and arrange them in a single layer at the base of the baking dish. Be cautious not to over-soak the biscuits as they may fall apart.

Spread half of the creamy mixture over the layer of lady fingers, smoothing it out evenly. Repeat the process of dipping the lady fingers into the coffee, layering them over the cream, and finishing with the remaining cream mixture spread evenly on top.

Dust generously with the cocoa powder and refrigerate for at least 2 hours, or preferably overnight, to allow the dessert to set properly before serving.

Tip: If you don't have icing sugar, you can blend granulated sugar into a fine powder.

SERVES 8–10

My younger sister introduced me to this dessert after living in Saudi Arabia for years. Every iftar she was invited to, there was always a version of it on the table. Some would add melted chocolate, others fruit, and occasionally soft cheese would be added. No two were exactly the same, but everyone loved it. You'll find versions of this dessert across many countries, each one slightly different, but the base stays the same. It's the biscuits; that's the thread that connects them all. So if you're going to make it, make sure to use Ulker or a good butter tea biscuit. The rest is flexible, but that part matters.

Biscuit Pudding

600 ml/2½ cups whipping or double (heavy) cream
½ x 397-g/14-oz can condensed milk
200 ml/1 scant cup evaporated milk
400g/14 oz Ulker or Petit Beurre biscuits (or any tea biscuits you prefer)
340 g/12 oz salted butter biscuits
1 tbsp cocoa powder

Equipment
20 x 15-cm/8 x 6-inch dish

Put the whipping cream and condensed milk in a bowl and whisk until thick and fluffy. Spread a thin layer of the whipped cream mixture on the bottom of the dish.

Pour the evaporated milk into a shallow bowl. Dunk the biscuits into the evaporated milk, ensuring they are lightly coated but not over-soaked as they may become too soft. Arrange the dipped biscuits in a single layer over the cream.

Spread another layer of whipped cream on top, then repeat the process of dunking the biscuits and layering cream. Continue creating layers until you have three to four layers, or more if desired.

Finish with a final layer of whipped cream and dust generously with the cocoa powder. Place the dish in the refrigerator to set for at least 2 hours, or up to 24 hours, to allow the layers to meld together for the best flavour and texture.

SERVES 8–10

There was a time my mum would soak dates in milk and fold them into her *doolsho* (see page 209), a small twist on the classic Somali cake. I couldn't tell you the measurements, and she hasn't made it like that in years, but it's the version I remember. Over time, in our home, that cake slowly evolved into what many of us now know as timir cake, something you'll find in Somali homes everywhere today. You will find it in just about every Somali restaurant dessert section – and for good reason. If you've ever had sticky toffee pudding, this is its close relative, just with a heavy hand of warm spices that really take it somewhere else. It's one of those desserts that appears every Ramadan, thanks to the abundance of dates. Sometimes, I like the cake on its own without the sauce. But let's be honest, the sauce is the deal-breaker. If you're skipping it, make sure to store the cake in an airtight container. It softens beautifully over a few days, and the flavour only gets better.

Timir Cake *Spiced Date Cake with Caramel Sauce*

3 tea bags
1 tsp Somali tea spice (see page 168)
300 ml/1¼ cups boiling water
400 g/14 oz Medjool dates, pitted
170 g/6 oz/¾ cup unsalted butter, softened
170 g/6 oz/generous ¾ cup caster (superfine) sugar
170 g/6 oz/generous ¾ cup dark soft brown sugar
4 large (US extra-large) eggs
340 g/12 oz/2½ cups self-raising (self-rising) flour
1 tsp ground cinnamon

For the caramel sauce
85 g/3 oz/6 tbsp unsalted butter
100 g/3½ oz/½ cup caster (superfine) sugar
100 g/3½ oz/½ cup dark soft brown sugar
225 ml/1 cup double (heavy) cream

Equipment
23-cm/9-inch Bundt tin, greased

Start by steeping the tea bags and the tea spice in the boiling water for at least 10 minutes until the tea is dark in colour. Pour this mixture over the dates and let them soak for 20 minutes to soften.

Preheat the oven to 180°C fan/200°C/400°F/gas mark 6.

In a large bowl, cream together the butter, caster sugar and dark brown sugar until smooth. Beat in the eggs one at a time, mixing well after each addition. Gradually fold in the flour until fully combined. This mixture is easily mixed by hand, but a handheld mixer works too.

Transfer the soaked dates and tea mixture to a blender and add the cinnamon. Blend until smooth (it's fine if some texture remains). Pour this date mixture into the flour mixture and stir until a smooth batter forms.

Pour the batter into the greased Bundt tin and bake in the preheated oven for about 45 minutes, or until a skewer inserted in the centre comes out clean.

For the caramel sauce, melt the butter in a saucepan over medium heat. Add the caster sugar and dark brown sugar and stir well. Gradually whisk in the cream and continue cooking until the sauce thickens, bubbles and reaches a rich caramel colour. Remove from the heat and set aside to cool slightly.

Once the cake has cooled, turn it onto a serving plate. Pour over the caramel sauce, or serve the cake as it is with the caramel sauce on the side.

MAKES ABOUT 80

When we think of *sambuus*, cheese isn't usually the first filling that comes to mind, but why not?! These are crisp, creamy and just sweet enough to sit perfectly on a Ramadan table. They're great for making in batches, ideally with company, because folding them is repetitive in the best way. You can shape them slightly larger if you prefer, but I like them mini. I like to freeze them before frying and take out a few at a time. Most of the time, I already have syrup lying around from *bur kuus kuus* (see page 38), so it all comes together without much effort. A little planning, a little folding and you've got something sweet to enjoy over the month.

Stuffed Sweet Cheese Samosas

1 tbsp plain (all-purpose) flour
1 packet pre-made samosa sheets (250 g/9 oz), you will need around 20-22 sheets
330 g/12 oz processed cheese triangles (I use Laughing Cow)
100 g/½ cup granulated sugar
4–5 cardamom pods
½ tsp lemon juice
sunflower oil, for frying
chopped pistachios, for sprinkling

Start by mixing the flour with 1 tablespoon of water in a small bowl until smooth.

Use a sharp knife to cut the samosa sheets into four long equal strips. Take one sheet (keep the remaining sheets covered with a kitchen towel) and place ⅓ teaspoon of cheese at one end. Fold the corner over to form a triangle, pressing down slightly to flatten the cheese. Continue folding the triangle over itself until you reach the end of the sheet. Dab a little flour paste on the end and press to seal the samosa. Repeat this process for the remaining samosas and cheese triangles, then place them in the freezer for at least 45 minutes until frozen.

Make the syrup by adding the sugar and cardamom to a saucepan with 125 ml/ ½ cup of water. Cook until it starts to boil, then add the lemon juice. Remove from the heat, remove the cardamom pods and set aside to cool.

Heat about 1 cm/ ½ inch sunflower oil, enough to shallow fry, in a pan over medium heat. Add the samosas in batches, trying not to overcrowd the pan. Fry for 1–2 minutes on one side until golden brown, then turn over and cook for another minute on the other side. Remove from the pan with a slotted spoon and place on paper towels to drain.

Place on a serving dish and, while hot, drizzle over the syrup and sprinkle with chopped pistachios.

SERVES 4-6

Basbousa is a simple, syrup-soaked semolina cake that never fails to please. Soft, slightly grainy and never too sweet, in my opinion, it's the kind of dessert that works for almost everyone. Popular across the Middle East and North Africa, with variations in every home, it's an easy win especially during Ramadan, and particularly when hosting.

Basbousa *Semolina Cake*

3 eggs
200 g/7 oz/1 cup granulated sugar
225 ml/1 cup sunflower oil
1 tsp vanilla bean paste
170 g/6 oz/1 cup coarse semolina
140 g/5 oz/1 cup self-raising (self-rising) flour
75 g/2½ oz/1 cup desiccated (dried unsweetened shredded) coconut, plus extra to serve
1 tsp baking powder
215 g/7½ oz/1 cup plain yogurt

For the syrup
200 g/7 oz/1 cup granulated sugar
1 tsp lemon juice
1 tsp orange or rose water (optional)

Equipment
32 x 22-cm/13 x 9-inch deep baking dish, well greased

Preheat the oven to 180°C fan/200°C/400°F/gas mark 6.

Beat the eggs in a large bowl. Add the sugar, oil and vanilla bean paste, whisking to combine. Gradually add the semolina, flour, desiccated coconut and baking powder. Switch to a wooden spoon and begin folding the mixture, then fold in the yogurt until well incorporated.

Spoon the batter into the greased baking dish; the mixture will be thick, so use the back of the spoon to spread it evenly toward the edges. Bake in the preheated oven for 20-25 minutes, or until golden brown around the edges.

While the cake bakes, prepare the syrup. In a saucepan over medium heat, combine the sugar and lemon juice with 285 ml/1¼ cups of water. Simmer gently, stirring until the sugar dissolves. Remove from the heat and stir in rose water or orange blossom water, if using.

Once the basbousa is baked, remove it from the oven and slice as desired while in the dish. Immediately pour the syrup evenly over the hot cake, adjusting the amount to your preference (you don't need to use it all).

Preheat the grill (broiler) to medium and grill (broil) the cake for 5 minutes, or until the top is golden brown. Finish by topping with extra desiccated coconut before serving.

MAKES 30

This is a simple spin on the classic cinnamon roll, using dates for the filling – something that just makes sense during Ramadan, when dates are everywhere. I've made them mini, partly for ease, but mostly to avoid overindulging. Just enough sweetness, and soft all the way through.

Mini Date Cinnamon Rolls

300 g/10½ oz date paste
150 ml/⅔ cup hot water
1 tbsp ground cinnamon
135 g/4½ oz/⅔ cup dark soft brown sugar
30 g/1 oz/2 tbsp unsalted butter, softened
75 ml/5 tbsp double (heavy) cream

For the dough
450 ml/scant 2 cups milk, lukewarm
20 g/¾ oz/2 tbsp fast-action dried yeast
150 g/5 oz/¾ cup granulated sugar
1 tsp ground cardamom
1 tsp salt
800 g/1 lb 12 oz/6 cups plain (all-purpose) flour, plus extra for dusting
140 g/5 oz/1¼ sticks unsalted butter, softened
sunflower or olive oil, for greasing

First, make the dough. In a large mixing bowl, combine the lukewarm milk and yeast, letting the yeast dissolve fully. Stir in the sugar, ground cardamom and salt until well mixed. Gradually add half of the flour, stirring until a smooth batter forms. Add the softened butter and mix in thoroughly. Gradually add the remaining flour, working until a soft dough begins to come together.

Turn the dough onto a floured surface, kneading until it's smooth and no longer sticky. Place the dough in a clean, lightly oiled bowl, cover with a kitchen towel and let it rise in a warm spot for about an hour, or until doubled in size.

While the dough rises, prepare the filling. Place the date paste in a bowl with 1–2 tablespoons of water and microwave for 30 seconds to soften. Gradually add the hot water in 50-ml/3½-tablespoon increments, mixing well after each addition. Stir in the cinnamon and set aside.

Mix in the softened butter and brown sugar. Once prepared, refrigerate the paste until the dough has risen, but no longer than 30 minutes.

Turn out the dough onto a well-floured surface and fold it over itself a few times. Divide the dough into three equal pieces. Roll one piece roughly into a 30 x 40-cm/12 x 16-inch rectangle.

Evenly spread one-third of the date mixture over the dough. Starting from a long side, roll the dough tightly into a log, pressing the edge to seal. Place it seam-side down and repeat with the remaining dough pieces. Use scissors to cut each log into ten equal pieces, making a total of 30 rolls.

Arrange the rolls in rows, flat-side down, on the prepared baking sheet. Cover and let them rise for another 15 minutes.

Meanwhile, preheat the oven to 180°C fan/200°C/400°F/gas mark 6.

For the cream cheese frosting

100 g/3½ oz/scant ½ cup cream cheese, room temperature

100 g/3½ oz/scant 1 cup icing (confectioners') sugar

15 g/½ oz/1 tbsp unsalted butter, softened

1 tbsp double (heavy) cream

½ tsp vanilla bean paste

Equipment

32 x 22-cm/13 x 9-inch baking dish

Evenly pour the double cream over the rolls. Bake the rolls on the middle shelf of the preheated oven for 20-25 minutes, rotating the tray halfway through for even browning. Once done, remove from the oven and allow them to cool in the tray for 15 minutes.

Prepare the frosting. In a bowl, mix the cream cheese and icing sugar until well combined. Add the butter, mixing until smooth and creamy. Stir in the double cream and vanilla until the frosting is silky.

Once the rolls have cooled slightly, spread one-third of the frosting over them with a spatula. Let them rest for 20 minutes, then spread the remaining frosting evenly over the tops before serving.

Tip: You can use soaked Medjool dates instead of date paste, if you prefer. Soak the dates in enough boiling water to cover for 30 minutes. Transfer the dates and their soaking water to a blender and blend until smooth. The paste should be thick but spreadable – add 1–2 tablespoons of hot water if needed, ensuring it doesn't become runny.

DESSERT

SERVES 8

It's 1997, and my parents have taken us to a Dubai that's unrecognizable from the bustling metropolis it is today. Below the apartment we're staying at, there's a little modest bakery that serves freshly baked *kunafa*. I can still remember the distinct aroma of the warm fresh cheese, lingering in my memory. I would beg my mum to take us, even in the squelching heat, just for one delicious slice of that *kunafa*.

I use low-moisture mozzarella cheese as a substitute for the more traditional akkawi cheese, and ricotta in place of ashta, commonly used in Arab countries.

Kunafa *Crispy Syrup-Soaked Pastry with Cream*

300 g/10½ oz kunafa dough
200 g/7 oz/1¾ sticks unsalted butter, melted
100 g/3½ oz/scant ½ cup ricotta
1 tbsp granulated sugar
1 tbsp milk (any milk will work)
250 g/9 oz/2¾ cups pre-grated mozzarella
200 g/7 oz/2 cups chopped pistachios

For the syrup
200 g/7 oz/1 cup granulated sugar
1 tbsp lemon juice
1 tsp rose water

Equipment
23-cm/9-inch round baking tin, well buttered

Preheat the oven to 200°C fan/220°C/425°F/gas mark 7.

In a large mixing bowl, cut the kunafa dough into 2.5-cm/1-inch pieces using scissors or your hands. Pour in the melted butter and mix well, ensuring all the strands are coated.

Add half the kunafa mixture to the greased tin, pressing it firmly with your fingers or the base of a cup to compact it into a solid layer.

In a blender, combine the ricotta, sugar and milk. Blend until smooth, then pour the mixture into the centre of the kunafa base, leaving a 2.5-cm/1-inch border around the edges. Spread the grated mozzarella evenly over the ricotta. Cover with the remaining kunafa dough, pressing down firmly and sealing the edges to create a dome-like shape.

Bake the kunafa in the preheated oven for 30–40 minutes, turning it halfway through, until golden brown and crisp.

To make the syrup, add the sugar and lemon juice to a saucepan with 285 ml/ 1¼ cups of water and place over medium heat. Cook for 5 minutes until it begins to bubble, then remove from the heat and stir in the rose water.

Remove the kunafa from the oven and immediately invert it onto a large plate. Pour three-quarters of the syrup evenly over the kunafa while it's still hot, you can pour the remainder over the individual portions. Sprinkle the chopped pistachios on top and serve.

SERVES 4

Whenever I make crème caramel, I can't help but think of my maternal aunt, *Allah yarhamha* (May God have mercy on her). It's one of those desserts that's quietly tied to her in my mind. Some dishes just carry memory like that. This version is gently infused with cardamom, which adds a subtle warmth to the silky custard. Feel free to cook the caramel to a deeper amber if you prefer a more intense, slightly bitter flavour.

Cardamom Crème Caramel

200 ml/1 scant cup milk
1 tsp vanilla bean paste
½ tsp ground cardamom
2 eggs, plus 2 egg yolks
35 g/1¼ oz/3 tbsp granulated sugar

For the caramel
75 g/2½ oz/6 tbsp granulated sugar

Equipment
4 x 160-ml/5½-fl oz ramekins, cups or glasses

Begin by making the caramel. Place a saucepan over medium-high heat and add the sugar and 90 ml/6 tablespoons of water. Allow the mixture to heat until it turns an amber colour – avoid stirring, but you can gently swirl the pan occasionally. Be cautious, as it can burn quickly once it starts to darken. Once ready, remove the pan from the heat and carefully pour the caramel into the ramekins or cups, ensuring it coats the bottoms evenly. Set aside.

Heat the milk in a saucepan until it is warm but not boiling. Remove from the heat, stir in the vanilla and cardamom, and set aside.

In a mixing bowl, whisk together the eggs, egg yolks and sugar until slightly fluffy. Gradually pour the warm milk into the egg mixture, whisking continuously to combine. Strain the custard through a sieve 2-3 times to ensure a smooth texture. Pour the strained mixture into the cups over the caramel layer and cover each cup tightly with aluminium foil.

Prepare a pot large enough to hold your cups or ramekins. Place a steaming rack inside the pot to keep the cups elevated from the base. Arrange the cups on the tray, ensuring they don't touch the sides or bottom of the pot. Add boiling water to the pot until it comes about two-thirds of the way up the sides of the cups. Cover the pot with a lid, leaving a small gap for air circulation – a skewer or wooden spoon can help balance the lid slightly open.

Steam over low heat for 40-45 minutes, then remove the cups and allow them to cool before refrigerating for at least 2 hours, or preferably overnight, to set fully. Serve chilled.

Drinks are never just about thirst. They are about comfort, about pause, about connection. Whether it's a warm cup shared in silence, or something cold and refreshing passed to a guest, drinks hold their own place on the table and in memory. They begin conversations, open meals and bring a sense of ease to the table.

I've always loved the Somali coffee *qaxwa* (see page 171): light, black and spiced just enough to wake your senses. Though it's deeply rooted in Somali culture, you'll also find variations of it across the Middle East. I usually drink it at the very start of iftar, right alongside my soup. There's something grounding about that combination: warm liquid, light spice, the slow easing into the evening after a day of fasting.

'Camel' milk (see page 181) also has a quiet presence in this chapter. It's another drink enjoyed across the Middle East, known for its creamy texture and slight sourness or saltiness. While it's not always easy to find, I've created a recipe here that comes close. A replica that still captures the feeling of it, even if not the exact taste. It's not something you drink often, which makes it feel special when you do.

Then there are the drinks made for fun, for hosting, for cooling down, for adding colour to the table. These are the ones that get poured into jugs with ice and fruit, or blended into something creamy and sweet. Some are refreshing, like watermelon mocktails (see page 174). Others, like my avocado smoothie (see page 178), are surprisingly filling. It's thick, nourishing and something I often reach for when I want something satisfying but simple.

This chapter is a mix of tradition and play. It holds the drinks I've grown up with, the ones I've come to love, and the ones I now make for family and guests. These recipes are made to sit beside every dish in this book – some perfect for suhoor, others to open your iftar, and a few that are ideal for celebrating and hosting on Eid. Whether warm or cold, light or rich, these drinks are here to comfort, to refresh and to bring people together, one glass at a time.

SERVES 2–3

There's a Somali proverb that says *shaah waa shaahid*, which translates to 'tea is a witness'. It's a reminder of how often tea is present during everyday moments, and the big ones too. And it's true. Tea is there for everything: from quiet pauses to guests dropping by and families gathered at iftar. It's often the first thing poured after dates and water, and the last thing sipped before the night winds down and prayers begin.

Shaah *Spiced Tea*

For the spice mix
5 green cardamom pods
8 cloves
1 small cinnamon stick

2 black tea bags (I use PG Tips)
2.5-cm/1-inch piece of fresh ginger, or ⅛ tsp ground ginger
125 ml/½ cup milk
125 ml/½ cup evaporated milk
3 tsp sugar

Begin by adding the cardamom, cloves and cinnamon to a pestle and mortar and gently crushing them to release their aroma.

In a small saucepan over medium heat, combine the teabags, crushed spices and 350 ml/1.5 cups of water.

If using fresh ginger, lightly crush it in the pestle and mortar and add it to the pan. If using ground ginger, stir it in.

Stir in the milk, evaporated milk and sugar, until well combined. Bring the mixture to a gentle boil, then reduce the heat to low and let it simmer until the tea develops a rich brown colour, around 5–6 minutes. Stir occasionally to prevent the milk from scorching.

Strain the tea into two mugs or three small cups, adjust the sweetness if necessary and serve immediately.

SERVES 4

In Somali, the word 'casariya' refers to afternoon tea or coffee time, and comes from 'casar', the name of the afternoon prayer, *casar* (*asr*), in Islam. *Casariya* is less about the food itself and more about the moment, an intangible cultural heritage. While both tea and coffee are often served, my own association has always been with *qaxwa* – a lightly spiced, sweet black coffee. When my daughter turned one, we took a long trip back home to Somalia. Every afternoon, just before the sun began to set, there would be a flask of *qaxwa* on the table out on the veranda, the ocean breeze drifting through – a quiet pause before the call to prayer. And it's the same feeling that comes just before breaking fast. Knowing there's something warm to sip, and a moment to settle before the prayer begins.

Qaxwa Somali (Qahwa) *Spiced Coffee*

¾ tsp ground cinnamon
2 tsp ground ginger
1½ tsp ground cardamom
3 tsp arabica coffee beans
sugar, to serve

Start by grinding the coffee beans in a spice grinder until they form a blended fine powder. Then add the cinnamon, ginger and cardamom, and pulse three to four times to combine the mixture until well blended. Transfer the qaxwa mixture to an airtight container and store in a cool, dry place. It will keep for up to six months.

When ready to prepare, add 650 ml/2.5 cups of water to a small saucepan over medium heat. Stir in 2 teaspoons of the qaxwa mixture and bring it to a gentle boil. Remove from the heat and pour the qaxwa into a flask or directly into serving cups. You may sieve (strain) the mixture for a clearer coffee, but I prefer not to, as the grounds will naturally settle at the bottom of the flask or cup. Sweeten with sugar to taste.

SERVES 6

Mint tea is something I always seem to make when people are over. It's simple, yes, but it has a way of making things feel a little more thoughtful. The scent of fresh mint, the clinking of glasses, the quiet pause it creates – it's a small ritual I've come to love. In some cultures, the higher the pour, the more respect you're showing, so don't be shy! Just be sure to fully submerge the mint while it steeps, or it'll turn brown. This one's as easy as they come, but it always does what it needs to.

Mint Tea

1½ tsp loose-leaf tea (such as Ceylon or Chinese gunpowder green tea)
8–9 sprigs mint
sugar, to serve

Bring 1.5 litres/6 cups of water to a rolling boil in a teapot or kettle. Add the tea and mint. Leave for 2 minutes on a rolling boil, then remove from the heat and leave to rest for 5 minutes.

Sieve (strain) into a teapot or serving cups and serve with sugar to taste. Traditionally, this tea is served quite sweet, but you can adjust the sweetness to your liking.

SERVES 2-4

No matter where I've spent Ramadan, there's always been mint lemonade nearby. Whether it was at my mum's, my own home, a friend's place or even a restaurant, it was always there. It doesn't need an invitation; it just shows up. Part of the ritual. Part of the table. I didn't grow up with fancy drinks or mocktails, but this one found its way in and stayed. There's something timeless about it. It just belongs. But if, for some reason, it's never made an appearance at yours, this is your sign to give it a go. The lemon brings the zing, the mint cools you down, and just enough sugar ties it all together. No fuss. No extras. Just the kind of refreshment that clears the palate, lifts your mood and brings a quiet kind of joy. Somehow, no matter who's around the table, everyone agrees on this one.

Mint Lemonade

4 lemons
handful mint, leaves picked
4 tbsp granulated sugar, or to taste
250–500 ml/1–2 cups sparkling water
ice cubes

Peel and quarter the lemons, discarding any seeds. Add the lemon flesh, mint and sugar to a blender. Blend until smooth, then strain the mixture to remove any pulp, ensuring a smooth finish.

Pour the strained juice into a jug (pitcher) filled with ice. Top up with sparkling water to taste, stir gently to combine, and serve immediately for a refreshing drink.

SERVES 2-3

Ramadan has fallen in the spring and summer for most of my life, so watermelon feels deeply tied to the season. My husband would take it upon himself to find the best one each year, flipping them over at the market, looking for that perfect yellow spot on the bottom. He never failed. This drink takes me right back to those warmer Ramadans. It's cold, sweet and so refreshing after a long fast. More than anything, it reminds me of that feeling – windows open, table set and that first sip of something ice cold.

Watermelon Mocktail

450 g/1 lb watermelon flesh
juice of 2 limes, plus lime slices and wedges to serve
2–3 sprigs mint, leaves picked, plus extra sprigs to serve
ice cubes (optional)
sparkling lemonade, chilled, to top up

Begin by chopping the watermelon into small chunks. Place the pieces in an airtight container or freezer bag and freeze for at least 12 hours.

When ready to make the mocktail, add the frozen watermelon, freshly squeezed lime juice and mint leaves to a blender. Pulse until the mixture becomes a slushy, granita-like texture. Be careful not to over-blend; you want some icy texture to remain.

When ready to serve, place a few mint leaves and a slice of lime at the bottom of a chilled glass and gently muddle them together. Add 125 ml/½ cup of the watermelon granita to the glass, along with a few ice cubes if desired. Pour chilled lemonade over the granita – just enough to lightly dissolve the mixture.

Finish with a garnish of fresh mint or a lime wedge, and serve immediately.

SERVES 4

There's something comforting about mango lassi. Maybe it's the way it pours thick and golden into a glass, or how the tang of yogurt meets the sweetness of mango just right. I also love how it blurs the line between drink and dessert – there's something playful about that, like it doesn't need to choose what it wants to be. I prefer to serve it after the main meal as it's rich enough to stand on its own and a little too heavy to start with after a long fast. It's thick enough to feel indulgent, but still light enough to sip easily. Cardamom is absolutely optional, but it's a spice that follows me through this book and through my kitchen. It's worth trying, if you haven't already.

Mango Lassi

3 mangos, peeled and chopped or 240 ml/1 cup canned mango pulp
2 tbsp granulated sugar (optional)
215 g/7½ oz/1 cup plain yogurt
250 ml/1 cup milk
¼ tsp ground cardamom (optional)
ice cubes (optional)

If using fresh mango, put it in a blender and blend, then taste to check the sweetness and add the sugar if needed.

Blend the mango pulp or blended fresh mango with the milk, yogurt and cardamom (if using) until the mixture is smooth and creamy. Pour over ice, if desired, and serve cold.

SERVES 2

Avocado drinks in some capacity are a shared cultural thread across the East African region and most likely beyond this region too. I personally had a lot of avocados growing up. I mean a *lot*. In salads, fruit salads and in smoothies. Avocados aren't grown in Somalia, but you wouldn't know it from how popular they are. You'll find them sold in markets across the country, often blended into sweet drinks rather than used in savoury dishes. Smoothies like this are especially common during Ramadan.

Avocado Smoothie

1 ripe avocado
200 ml/1 scant cup milk (any milk will work)
2 tbsp Greek yogurt
1–2 tbsp condensed milk, to taste
ice cubes

Start by scooping the avocado flesh into a blender, discarding the skin and stone (pit). Add the milk, Greek yogurt and condensed milk. Blend until smooth and creamy. Pour into a glass and serve with ice cubes.

SERVES 4

'Camel' milk may be unfamiliar to many, but it carries deep cultural significance. Its roots trace back to the time of the Prophet Muhammad (peace be upon him). In countries such as Saudi Arabia, the UAE, Oman and Qatar, camel milk has long been a staple, particularly vital for Bedouin communities living in the desert. While it's nearly impossible to find where I live now, this drink is, for me, more about nostalgia than anything else.

'Camel' Milk

450 g/1 lb/2 cups plain yogurt
500 ml/2 cups lemon-lime soda (such as 7up or Sprite)

In a large jug (pitcher), whisk the yogurt until smooth and creamy. Pour in 125 ml/½ cup of the lemon-lime soda, stirring well to combine. Gradually add the remaining soda, mixing gently until fully incorporated. Serve immediately, chilled, and enjoy.

After a month of patience, prayer and reflection, Eid arrives like sunlight breaking through. The air feels different. The house feels different. There's a sense of joy that hums through everything, from the early morning buzz to the scent of something sweet baking in the kitchen.

Eid is a day of festivity, a day of joy. It's bright, full of life, and carries celebration with it. The day always begins early, long before the table is laid. We get dressed and head to the mosque for the Eid prayer. The atmosphere is full of energy. People greeting one another, sweets being handed out, children weaving through the crowd in their new clothes. There's a buzz in the air, a feeling that the celebration has already begun. You can feel the joy before you even return home.

When we return home, we sit down for a breakfast that's as much tradition as it is comfort. Dishes like *fuul* and *suqaar*, which appear in the Mains chapter of this book, often find their way to the table. It's the first breakfast in a month that doesn't carry the weight of fasting, and somehow, it always feels like the most nourishing meal of all.

Later in the day, the main event takes shape. Dishes like *surbiyan* (see page 192), *kabsa* (see page 212), and slow-cooked lamb shoulder (see page 204) take centre stage and are made to be shared. And then there are those special plates that only appear on Eid, like *cambaabur*, a soft and spiced pancake (see page 203), a dish I wait for all year long. These aren't everyday recipes, they're saved for something special, and that's exactly what Eid is. Food becomes the way we connect all day long. We take dishes to family members' homes or open our own doors to guests. Plates are passed between households, leftovers are packed with care, and the spirit of giving continues, just in a different form. It's not about perfection, it's about presence. Feeding others, being fed, and being together.

This chapter is a celebration of all the meals that make Eid feel like Eid. Some recipes are nostalgic, others newer, but all are made with love, and meant to be shared. However you mark the day, I hope these dishes add warmth, sweetness, and something truly festive to your table and to those you share it with.

Za'atar Focaccia

SERVES 10–12

Since becoming a mum, I've developed a bit of a soft spot (or maybe a full-blown obsession) for bread making – usually with my little sous chef (my toddler) by my side. Focaccia is the one we've really perfected over time. It's forgiving, satisfying and somehow feels like more than just bread when you get it right. You'll know exactly what I mean when you make it. Topping it with za'atar just makes sense. The mix of herbs and sesame pairs beautifully with the olive oil-rich dough, adding a sharp, earthy flavour that turns a simple tray of bread into something special. Serve it on its own (as it absolutely holds its own) or alongside your favourite dish.

420 ml/1¾ cups lukewarm water
7-g/¼-oz sachet fast-action dried yeast
1 tbsp honey
2 tsp salt
2–3 tbsp olive oil, plus extra for drizzling
500 g/1 lb 2 oz/3½ cups strong white bread flour
2 tbsp za'atar
flaky sea salt

Equipment
23 x 30-cm/9 x 12-inch baking tray, lined

In a large bowl, combine the water, yeast, honey and salt. Mix thoroughly until the yeast dissolves. Add the flour and mix until a sticky dough forms, scraping down the sides of the bowl as needed. Shape the dough into a rough ball, cover the bowl and let it rest for 30 minutes.

Wet your hands and begin folding the dough. Pull one side of the dough up and fold it towards the centre, repeating this process 3–4 times. Cover the bowl and let the dough rest for another 20 minutes.

Repeat the folding process; this time, the dough will feel smoother and easier to handle. Once folded, turn the dough smooth-side up and place it in an airtight container. Drizzle a little olive oil over the dough and rub it gently to coat. Cover and refrigerate overnight, or up to 2 days.

When ready to bake, remove the dough from the fridge. It should have risen significantly. Drizzle 2–3 tablespoons of olive oil over the lined baking tray, spreading it evenly. Turn the dough out onto the tray. Rub your hands with some of the oil from the tray, then gently stretch one side of the dough over itself, repeating with the opposite side. Turn the dough so it sits lengthways in the tray and then turn the dough smooth-side up. Cover and leave to rise for 2 hours, or until it has doubled in size. The rising time will vary depending on the temperature of your space.

Once risen, use oiled fingers to gently stretch the dough toward the edges of the tray.

Preheat the oven to 220°C fan/240°C/475°F/gas mark 9.

Drizzle more olive oil over the dough and sprinkle with the za'atar. Use your fingers to press dimples all over the surface of the dough. Finish with a scattering of flaky sea salt.

Bake on the lowest rack of your oven for 20–22 minutes, or until golden brown.

Allow the focaccia to cool slightly before slicing and serving.

MAKES 55–65

Kac kac is one of those snacks that always signals a celebration. Crisp and lightly spiced, they sit somewhere between a cake and a biscuit, and are best eaten with a cup of tea or black *qaxwa* (see page 171). Whenever I visit Somalia, I always request a batch because there is nothing like having them hot, straight from the oil, with coffee in hand. They're simple but nostalgic – the scent of cardamom always takes me straight back to Eid mornings, when tins of *kac kac* would appear alongside other sweets, ready for whoever came through the door. They keep well, but they rarely get the chance.

Kac Kac (Ka' Ka') *Fried Biscuits*

280 g/10 oz/2 cups plain (all-purpose) flour
100 g/3½ oz/½ cup granulated sugar
1 tsp baking powder
1 tbsp ground cardamom
2 eggs
115 g/4 oz/½ cup ghee or unsalted butter, melted
sunflower oil, for frying

Combine the flour, sugar, baking powder and ground cardamom in a large bowl, mixing well to distribute the ingredients evenly.

In a separate bowl, beat the eggs.

Make a well in the centre of the flour mixture and pour in the beaten eggs and melted ghee or butter. Begin mixing with a spoon until a dough starts to form.

Knead the dough in the bowl for 3–4 minutes, until smooth. Cover and let it rest for 30 minutes.

Once rested, roll out the dough to a rectangle around 26 x 34 cm/ 10 x 13 inch, and 1 cm thick. Using a sharp knife or pastry cutter, slice 10 lines lengthways, then cut 8 lines diagonally across to form diamond shapes. You can create more lines for smaller biscuits.

Heat the oil in a pan until it reaches 180°C/350°F, or until a cube of bread browns in 30 seconds. Carefully add the dough pieces, working in batches and turning them frequently to ensure even cooking, and fry until deep golden brown.

Remove using a slotted spoon and transfer to paper towels to absorb any excess oil. These biscuits can be stored in an airtight container for up to a week.

SERVES 4–6

Catriyat, for me, is deeply tied to celebration. It's made with vermicelli noodles, gently fried in ghee until golden, then tossed with sugar, cardamom and sometimes a handful of raisins or nuts. The result is soft, lightly spiced and just sweet enough. Growing up, I only ever saw it during Eid or when guests were over – a quiet sign that something special was happening. It pairs perfectly with a cup of *shaah* (see page 168) or *qaxwa* (see page 171), and, if you like, you can serve it with a splash of milk or cream.

Cadriyat (Adriyat) *Sweetened Vermicelli*

200 g/7 oz vermicelli
2 tbsp ghee
60 g/5 tbsp sugar
10 cardamom pods, crushed
70 g/2½ oz/½ cup raisins
  (optional)

Begin by crushing the vermicelli directly in its packaging to create small shards. Heat a frying pan (skillet) over medium heat and add the crushed vermicelli. Stir in the ghee, ensuring each piece is well coated. Cook, stirring frequently, until the vermicelli turns golden brown. Be careful not to let it burn.

In a separate small saucepan over medium heat, add the sugar, cardamom pods and 500 ml/2 cups of water. Stir to dissolve the sugar and bring the mixture to a gentle boil.

Pour the boiling syrup into the pan with the vermicelli and stir well to combine. If desired, add raisins at this stage and mix them through. Continue to stir and cook for another 5 minutes to allow the flavours to meld. Remove from the heat and serve immediately.

SERVES 6

This is a fragrant rice and meat dish with deep roots in Yemeni cuisine. It's a close cousin to biryani, with its method of slow cooking and layering. Through migration and trade, it made its way into Somali cuisine. Over time, *surbiyan* (or *zurbian*) has become a familiar celebratory dish in Somali homes, especially during weddings, large gatherings and Eid. This dish requires patience, and from the marinade to the broth, every part of it is intentional. Each step builds into something rich and layered, and, when it all comes together, it's close to perfection. It's not essential, but if you want that restaurant-style finish, before leaving to rest, place a small ramekin with a splash of oil or ghee inside the pot, drop in a piece of hot coal, and immediately seal with foil to trap in the smoke. It leaves behind the most beautiful depth and aroma, just enough to make the whole dish sing.

Surbiyan *One-Pot Lamb Rice*

1 kg/2 lb 4 oz lamb shoulder on the bone, meat diced
1 tsp Vegeta or all-purpose seasoning
1½ tsp xawaash (see page 142)
125 ml/½ cup tamarind paste
200 ml/1 scant cup sunflower oil
1 large onion, sliced
1 green finger chilli (chile), top removed, seeds left in
1 key lime, halved
100 g/3½ oz/7 tbsp plain yogurt
4 garlic cloves
small handful fresh coriander (cilantro)
1 tomato
½ tsp ground cardamom
2 cinnamon sticks
2 chicken or vegetable stock cubes
600 g/1 lb 5 oz/3 cups basmati rice (I use sella basmati)
90 g/3 oz/½ cup sultanas (golden raisins)
⅓ tsp powdered green food colouring
⅓ tsp powdered orange food colouring
1 tsp distilled white vinegar

Put the lamb in a bowl and add the Vegeta seasoning, xawaash and tamarind. Use your hands to coat the meat all over.

Add the oil to a large pot over medium heat. When hot, add the sliced onions and cook until brown. Keep an eye as we want them crispy but not burnt. Remove the onions and leave to drain on a paper towel. Remove most of the oil and reserve for later use.

Add the marinated lamb into the same pot and cook until brown. Add the chilli. Leave to cook on medium heat for 5 minutes. Squeeze in the lime juice and throw the squeezed lime halves into the pot.

In a blender, combine 3 tablespoons of the yogurt, the garlic cloves, coriander and about 50 g/½ cup of the fried onions. Blend until smooth. Pour half the blended mixture into the meat and leave to cook for 5 minutes. Add 100 ml/6½ tablespoons of the reserved oil to the meat and continue to cook.

To the remaining blended mixture, add the tomato, cardamom and 2 more tablespoons of the yogurt; blend until smooth. Pour this mixture into the meat to cook for 10 minutes.

Pour in 225 ml/1 cup of water, mix well, then cover with a lid and continue to simmer on medium-low heat for 20 minutes.

Meanwhile, bring a pot of water to the boil for the rice. Add the cinnamon sticks and the stock cubes, then add the rice. Cook for about 7 minutes until parboiled (the grains should be elongated and soft on the outside, but still firm in the centre), then drain.

Carefully layer the rice over the meat in the pot, then shake the pot gently to get an even layer (ensure the layers remain distinct; do not mix the meat with the rice). Create a few holes on the rice and add ½ teaspoon yogurt into each. Scatter the sultanas on one side, the remaining fried onions in another. Add the food colouring in two corners and drizzle the vinegar over the food colouring to enhance its colour and vibrancy. Pour 3-4 tablespoons of the remaining oil on top of everything. Cover the pot tightly with foil and place the lid on.

Cook over medium heat until steam escapes from the lid, then reduce to the lowest heat and cook for 15 minutes. Leave the dish to rest before serving.

To serve, use a large spoon to scoop from the bottom to the top, mixing the layers together.

SERVES 8

This tart is exactly what the name suggests – a little bit baklava, a little bit custard – and every bite completely worth it. Crisp, golden layers of filo filled with a smooth, lightly sweetened custard, then topped with warm syrup and crushed nuts. It's not traditional in any sense, but it still feels familiar.

Inspired by the flavours of baklava, but softened with something creamy and comforting, it's best served warm when the syrup is still glossy and the filo crackles under your fork.

Baklava Custard Tart

150 g/5 oz/⅔ cup unsalted butter
14–16 filo (phyllo) pastry sheets

For the filling
350 ml/1½ cups milk
50 ml/3½ tbsp double (heavy) cream
2 tbsp cornflour (cornstarch)
50 g/1¾ oz/¼ cup caster (superfine) sugar
1 tbsp vanilla bean paste
2 egg yolks

For the syrup
250 g/9 oz granulated sugar
3–4 cardamom pods, slightly cracked open
2 tbsp orange blossom water
3 tbsp lemon juice

For the topping
50 g/1¾ oz/½ cup crushed pistachios
flaky sea salt

Equipment
32 x 22-cm/13 x 9-inch baking dish

Preheat the oven to 190°C fan/210°C/415°F/gas mark 6–7.

Start by making the filling. In a pan over low heat, bring the milk and cream to a simmer, then remove from the heat. In a bowl, whisk the cornflour, sugar, vanilla and egg yolks until smooth, then pour into the saucepan. Cook over medium heat for 5 minutes, stirring continuously until thick.

Next, melt the butter. We want it in pure liquid form.

Brush a layer of the melted butter to cover the base and sides of the baking dish. Place a sheet of filo pastry in the buttered dish, pressing gently to ensure it sticks to the butter. Repeat this process for 6–7 layers, overlapping the sheets so they cover the base of the dish and come up the sides.

Pour the prepared custard filling evenly over the filo layers. Fold the edges of the filo over the custard, trimming any excess pastry if necessary to fit the dish. Brush another layer of butter over the folded sides, then place a new sheet of filo on top. You may need to cut the sheets to fit your dish. Continue layering with 5–6 more sheets, making sure to brush butter between each layer. Make sure the final layer is well-buttered.

Cut the pastry into slices according to your preference. It is easier to cut the pastry whilst it is soft before it bakes and becomes crispy. I like to cut it into eight pieces. Bake in the preheated oven for 20 minutes, or until the top is golden brown and crisp.

While the pastry is baking, prepare the syrup. Combine all the syrup ingredients with 150 ml/⅔ cup of water in a pan over medium heat and simmer until the sugar dissolves. Remember to remove the cardamom pods before serving.

Once the pastry is golden, remove from the oven and immediately pour the syrup over it. If you'd like more syrup when serving, simply double the recipe. Immediately add the chopped pistachios and scattering of flaky sea salt and serve.

SERVES 10–14

Khaliat nahal, which means 'honeycomb' in Arabic, is a soft, sweet yeasted bread known for its signature shape. You'll find versions of it across the Middle East, always filled with cheese and finished with a syrup that changes depending on the kitchen it came from, but the share-and-tear nature of it is always the same. The first time I had it was at a neighbour's house during Ramadan. I must've been around twelve. The tray hit the table and disappeared in minutes, everyone pulling off pieces, syrup running down their fingers. I remember asking for more, hoping there was another batch tucked away. Every Ramadan after that, I'd wait excitedly for her to make it again, right up until we moved away. Eventually, I took it upon myself to learn. And over time, I've perfected it to be exactly how I remembered: incredibly soft, pillowy and impossible to stop picking at.

Khaliat Nahal *Honeycomb Bread*

125 ml/½ cup milk
125 ml/½ cup evaporated milk, warmed
1 tbsp honey
1 tbsp fast-action dried yeast
2 large (US extra-large) eggs
50 g/1¾ oz/3½ tbsp unsalted butter, softened, plus extra for greasing
400 g/14 oz/3 cups plain (all-purpose) flour, plus extra for dusting and if needed
25 g/1 oz/¼ cup powdered milk (I use Nido)
neutral oil, for drizzling
170 g/6 oz/¾ cup cream cheese, room temperature
125–175 ml/½–¾ cup condensed milk, for drizzling

For the glaze
100 g/3½ oz/½ cup granulated sugar
4–5 crushed cardamom pods
1 tbsp honey

Equipment
23-cm/9-inch round baking dish, greased

Pour the milk, evaporated milk, honey and yeast into a large mixing bowl. Whisk well and leave the mixture to sit for 10 minutes to let the yeast activate.

Beat one of the eggs and add to the yeast mixture. Mix thoroughly. Add the softened butter and mix until incorporated. Gradually add the flour and powdered milk, stirring until a rough dough forms. The dough may feel sticky; that is ok.

Transfer it to a lightly floured surface and knead for about 10 minutes until it becomes smooth and elastic. If needed, add an extra tablespoon of flour and knead further.

Shape the dough into a ball, lightly coat it with oil, and place it in a greased bowl. Cover and leave the dough in a warm spot for about 1 hour, or until doubled in size.

Preheat the oven to 180°C fan/200°C/400°F/gas mark 6.

Once ready, turn the dough onto a lightly floured surface and divide it into 37 equal pieces, weighing about 20 g/⅔ oz each. As you work, keep the balls covered with a kitchen towel.

Press one piece into a small flat circle, place a small piece of cream cheese in the centre, and seal it back into a ball. Set aside under the kitchen towel and repeat with the remaining dough and cream cheese.

Recipe continues overleaf

Place one dough ball in the centre of the greased baking dish, then arrange three on each side of it to form a row of seven. Above this row, place six, then five, then four. Repeat the same pattern below the centre row to create a honeycomb shape. Alternatively, start with one ball in the middle, then surround it with six, followed by 12, then 18, filling the pan. Any small gaps will close as the dough rises and bakes.

In a small bowl, whisk the second egg with 1 tablespoon of water and brush this egg wash over the buns.

Bake in the preheated oven for 20 minutes, applying a second layer of egg wash halfway through cooking, and rotating the dish for an even bake.

While the bread bakes, make the glaze by adding the sugar and crushed cardamom pods to a saucepan with 125 ml/½ cup of water. Bring to the boil, stir in the honey and remove from the heat to cool slightly. Strain out the cardamom seeds.

Remove the buns from the oven and, while still hot, pour half to three-quarters of the syrup over them, adjusting the amount according to preference. Follow with a drizzle of condensed milk. The bread is best served warm, with the remaining glaze and condensed milk added on serving, if needed.

SERVES 6

Every Eid, my mum or my brother-in-law would pick up a few pieces from the bakery, tucked in a box next to *xalwo*, a glossy spiced jelly cut into diamonds, and *qumbe*, a sweet coconut crumb that melts the second it hits your tongue. *Nac nac loos* looks like the kind of sweet that might test your teeth, but I promise you, it's not. It's light, just the right kind of crunchy, with a chew that keeps you reaching back for more. And the best part? It's actually very simple to make. Just sugar, peanuts and a little patience. For a deeper flavour, let the sugar darken into a rich amber before stirring in the peanuts.

Nac Nac Loos (Na' Na') *Peanut Brittle*

200 g/1 cup sugar
30 g/1 oz/ 2 tbsp unsalted butter, softened
135 g/4½ oz/1 cup roasted peanuts
½ tsp salt (if using unsalted peanuts)

Equipment
baking sheet, lined

In a medium saucepan over medium-low heat, add the sugar and cook, stirring gently, until it dissolves. Once dissolved, stop stirring and allow the mixture to boil. When the sugar turns a light golden colour, add the butter. As soon as the butter melts, stir in the peanuts and salt (if using), ensuring they are evenly coated. Continue cooking, stirring occasionally, until the mixture reaches a deep golden-brown colour.

Immediately pour the brittle onto the prepared baking sheet and spread it into an even layer with a spatula or the back of a spoon. Work quickly as the brittle sets fast. For a smoother finish, gently roll over the brittle with a rolling pin.

Let the brittle cool completely at room temperature for 30–45 minutes. Once hardened, break it into pieces using your hands or a knife.

Store the brittle in an airtight container at room temperature for up to 2 weeks.

MAKES 8–10

Cambaabur are thin, fermented pancakes, similar to *laxoox* (see page 117), but with a distinct flavour. Lightly spiced and slightly tangy, they're usually reserved for Eid and rarely served outside of it. Every year, my mum's friend and neighbour would drop off a stack, still warm, and it became something we quietly looked forward to. Serve with a loose yogurt on the side. They're best left covered for about 30 minutes before eating to let everything settle.

Cambaabur (Ambaabur) *Spiced and Sweetened Fermented Pancakes*

280 g/10 oz/2 cups plain (all-purpose) flour
70 g/2½ oz/½ cup self-raising (self-rising) flour
140 g/5 oz/1 cup sorghum
1½ tsp fast-action dried yeast
2 tsp granulated sugar, plus extra for sprinkling
1¼ tsp salt
750 ml/3 cups warm water
2 tsp fennel seeds
1 tsp cumin seeds
1 tsp nigella seeds
2–3 garlic cloves
1 small onion
1½ tsp ground turmeric
sunflower oil, for frying
plain yogurt, to serve

Start by adding the plain flour, self-raising flour, sorghum, yeast, sugar and salt to a bowl. Stir to combine. Gradually pour in the warm water, whisking vigorously to form a smooth batter.

Grind the fennel, cumin and nigella seeds using a grinder or pestle and mortar. Add the ground seeds to a blender along with the garlic and onion, and blend into a paste. Add 1–2 tablespoons of water if needed to help blend.

Pour this paste into the flour mixture and stir to combine. The batter should be smooth, with no lumps. If needed, blend the entire mixture for a few seconds to ensure a smooth consistency. Stir in the ground turmeric and mix well.

Cover the bowl and refrigerate overnight to ferment. If you're short on time, a few hours will suffice, but the longer it rests, the better the flavour.

Once ready to cook, remove the mixture from the fridge. It should have risen slightly, with air pockets on the surface.

Heat a non-stick frying pan (skillet) over medium heat. Drizzle a teaspoon of oil into the pan and immediately use a folded paper towel to remove any excess oil. The pan should be lightly oiled, but not have visible drops of oil.

Take a ladle and pour one ladleful of the batter into the pan. Use your other hand to tilt the pan slightly, so the batter spreads to the edges. The batter should be slightly thick like a flatbread rather than thin like a crêpe. Let it cook until small air pockets start to form. Once the surface appears dry, brush with oil and sprinkle a teaspoon of sugar over the top. Check the underside is golden brown, then flip it over. Cook for 1 minute until the underside is caramelized and golden brown, then remove the cambaabur from the pan and place it on a plate. Repeat the process until all the batter is used.

Pile the cambaabur on a plate and let them rest for at least 1 hour before serving with yogurt.

SERVES 5-6

Roasted lamb shoulder is my favourite part of any celebratory meal. The crispy edges, the tender meat that pulls apart with a spoon. I always look forward to it, no matter what else is on the table. The marinade can be made ahead of time, which makes things easier when you're hosting or cooking for a crowd. It becomes the centrepiece of any Eid table without even trying.

Roasted Lamb Shoulder

¼ green (bell) pepper
1 small red onion
2 tsp plain yogurt
1 tomato
4 garlic cloves
small handful fresh coriander (cilantro)
1.5 kg/3 lb 5 oz lamb shoulder on the bone
2 tbsp sunflower oil
1 tsp tamarind paste
1 tsp ground cumin
1 heaping tsp ground coriander
1 tsp curry powder
½ tsp coarsely ground black pepper
1½ tsp Vegeta or all-purpose seasoning

In a blender, combine the green pepper, red onion, yogurt, tomato, garlic cloves and fresh coriander. Blend until smooth.

Prepare the lamb by cutting deep slits on both sides. In a bowl, mix the oil, tamarind paste, cumin, ground coriander, curry powder, black pepper and Vegeta seasoning into a thick marinade. Rub this mixture thoroughly over the lamb, ensuring it gets into the slits and coats both sides evenly. Pour half of the blended sauce over the lamb, ensuring an even coating, and let it marinate for at least 30 minutes – longer if possible for deeper flavour.

Preheat the oven to 200°C fan/220°C/425°F/gas mark 7.

Place the lamb in a baking dish, cover with foil to ensure no air can enter and roast in the preheated oven for 1 hour and 20 minutes. Remove the foil, pour the remaining blended sauce over the lamb, and spoon any pan juices on top. Turn on the grill (broiler) setting and cook for an additional 5 minutes on each side to achieve a slightly charred finish.

SERVES 8–10

Doolsho is the kind of cake that quietly lives in the background of so many Somali homes. A simple pound cake, lightly spiced, soft and sweet, always sitting in a container on the kitchen counter. My mum would make it at least once a month, sometimes twice. I remember always wanting the first slice straight from the oven, burning my fingers as I walked away. We'd eat it just as it was, dipped into a cup of *shaah*, or covered in freshly made hot cardamom custard. The custard is smooth, gently spiced and honestly good enough to eat on its own with a spoon.

Doolsho Somali and Cardamom Custard
Spiced Pound Cake with Cardamom Custard

4 eggs
200 g/7 oz/1 cup granulated sugar
140 g/5 oz/1 cup self-raising (self-rising) flour
2 tbsp milk (any milk will work)
2 tbsp sunflower oil
⅓ tsp ground cardamom

For the custard
3 egg yolks
60 g/2 oz/⅓ cup granulated sugar
400 ml/1¾ cups milk (any milk will work)
1 tsp vanilla bean paste
½ tsp ground cardamom
25 g/1 oz/¼ cup cornflour (cornstarch)
200 ml/scant 1 cup double (heavy) cream

Equipment
23-cm/9-inch Bundt tin, greased

Preheat the oven to 180°C fan/200°C/400°F/gas mark 6.

Start by separating the four egg yolks from the whites. In a mixing bowl, whisk the egg whites until soft peaks form. Gradually add the sugar while whisking, ensuring the mixture becomes glossy and smooth. Gently fold in the egg yolks, followed by the flour, using a spatula to maintain the airiness of the batter. Add the milk and oil, folding gently to combine. Finally, fold in the cardamom.

Pour the batter into the greased Bundt tin. Tap the tin a few times on the counter to release any air bubbles. Bake in the preheated oven for 30 minutes, or until golden brown and a skewer inserted in the centre comes out clean. Allow to cool for 10 minutes in the tin, then turn out onto a wire rack to cool completely.

Meanwhile, make the custard. Add the egg yolks and sugar to a mixing bowl, and whisk until smooth. In a saucepan, heat 300 ml/1¼ cups of the milk with the vanilla over medium heat. Once it begins to simmer, remove from the heat. Add the cardamom, stir, and let the mixture rest for 10 minutes.

In a separate bowl, whisk the remaining milk with the cornflour until smooth, then combine this mixture with the egg mixture, stirring well to ensure a smooth blend.

Return the mixture to the saucepan and bring it to a gentle boil, stirring continuously as it thickens quickly. Once the custard is thick and smooth, remove from the heat. Add the double cream and stir until fully incorporated.

Once the cake has cooled slightly, slice into portions and serve warm, generously drizzled with the hot custard.

MAKES 12–14

Also known as *atayef* or *katayef*, this dish has a long and rich history in the Arab world, especially as a Ramadan dessert. The name *qatayef* refers to the batter itself – similar to a yeasted pancake, but cooked on only one side. Don't flip them, and don't be tempted to rush. Wait until the surface is full of bubbles and completely dry before lifting them off the pan. That's what gives them their signature texture. Once cooked, the pancakes are typically filled with crushed nuts, akkawi cheese or cream, then either folded and served as-is, or deep-fried and soaked in sugar syrup. The fact that they only appear during Ramadan gives them a special, nostalgic status. They're not just dessert, they signal the spirit of the season.

Qatayef *Cheese-Filled, Syrup-Soaked Sweet Pancakes*

200 g/7 oz/1½ cups plain (all-purpose) flour
170 g/6 oz/1 cup semolina
1 tbsp powdered milk
1 tsp flaxseed
2 tbsp granulated sugar
1 tbsp baking powder
½ tsp salt
½ tsp fast-action dried yeast
750 ml/3 cups lukewarm water
200 g/7 oz low-moisture mozzarella or akkawi cheese
200 ml/scant 1 cup sunflower oil
crushed pistachios, for sprinkling

For the syrup
400 g/2 cups granulated sugar
1 tsp lemon juice
1 tsp orange blossom or rose water (optional)

Directly into a blender or food processor, add the flour, semolina, powdered milk, flaxseed, sugar, baking powder, salt and yeast. Mix briefly to combine. Pour in the water and blend until the batter is smooth and lump-free. If using a mixing bowl, use a hand blender to achieve a similar consistency. The batter should have a slightly thick but pourable texture. Cover and leave the batter to ferment for 30 minutes–1 hour.

Once fermented, blend the batter again briefly to ensure smoothness.

Heat a non-stick frying pan (skillet) over medium heat. Add a small dash of oil to the pan, then use a piece of paper towel to wipe it evenly across the surface, leaving the pan lightly greased.

Using a ladle or 125 ml/½ cup measure, slowly pour batter into the pan to form a circle about 10 cm/4 inches in diameter. As the pancake cooks, you'll see bubbles forming on the surface and the batter will change colour, becoming fully opaque and dry on top. The underside should have a nice golden colour. Do not flip the pancake. Once the surface is set and dry, remove the pancake and place it on a plate lined with paper towels. Cover the plate with a clean towel to keep the pancake soft. Repeat with the remaining batter.

To fill, place 1 tablespoon of cheese in the centre of a pancake. You may need less depending on the size of the pancake. Fold it in half and firmly press the edges to seal. Ensure the edges are well sealed to prevent leaks during frying. Do not overfill. Repeat with the remaining pancakes.

To make the syrup, add the sugar, lemon juice and 250 ml/1 cup of water to a pan. Bring to a gentle simmer over medium heat, stirring until the sugar dissolves completely. Remove from the heat. If using rose water or orange blossom water, stir it in after removing the syrup from the heat. Set aside to cool slightly.

Heat the sunflower oil in a shallow frying pan (skillet) or small pot over medium heat until it reaches 180°C/350°F, or until a cube of bread browns in 30 seconds. Add the qatayef, in batches, frying for about 1 minute on each side until they are a light golden brown. Avoid overcrowding the pan.

Remove the fried qatayef with a slotted spoon and place them on a plate lined with paper towels to absorb any excess oil.

While still warm, dip each qatayef into the sugar syrup, ensuring they are fully coated. Place the coated qatayef on a serving plate and sprinkle with crushed pistachios. Serve immediately while warm.

SERVES 6–8

This version of *kabsa* was inspired by a recent trip to perform Umrah (Islamic pilgrimage) in Saudi Arabia. The rice is spiced and deeply fragrant, cooked with tender chicken until everything comes together in one pot. It's the kind of dish that fills the table and feels special without needing much else.

Saudi Kabsa *Saudi Spiced Rice with Chicken*

6 tbsp ghee or sunflower oil
1 white onion, finely chopped
1 carrot, grated
2 cinnamon sticks
6 cardamom pods, crushed
6 cloves
1 star anise
2 dried limes
4 bay leaves
1 tsp black pepper
½ tsp salt
½ tsp ground cinnamon
1 tsp garlic powder
⅛ tsp celery salt
½ tsp ground ginger
1 tsp paprika
½ tsp ground turmeric
½ tsp dried lime powder
1 tsp Aleppo pepper
1½ tsp ground coriander
1½ tsp ground cumin
2 chicken stock cubes
1 whole baby chicken, halved
400 g/14 oz/2 cups basmati rice (I use sella basmati)
4 tbsp flaked (sliced) almonds
2 tbsp raisins or sultanas (golden raisins)

Tip: This pairs great with Somali *bisbaas cagaar* (see page 141) or *shidni* (see page 138).

Start by heating 4 tablespoons of the ghee or sunflower oil in a deep pot over medium–high heat. Add the chopped onion and grated carrot, cooking for 2–3 minutes until softened. Stir in the cinnamon sticks, crushed cardamom pods, cloves, star anise, dried limes and bay leaves, ensuring they are coated in the oil. Add the black pepper, salt, ground cinnamon, garlic powder, celery salt, ginger, paprika, turmeric, lime powder, Aleppo pepper, coriander and cumin. Stir well to combine and release the spices' aromas. Crumble in 1 chicken stock cube and mix before adding the halved baby chicken. Turn the chicken in the pot to ensure it is well coated in the spice mixture. Pour in 500 ml/2 cups of water, place the chicken meat-side down, and leave to cook for 10 minutes with the lid on.

Meanwhile, preheat the oven to 190°C fan/210°C/410°F/gas mark 7.

Wash the rice thoroughly, then place it in a bowl and cover with boiling water. Leave it to soak for at least 20 minutes.

Remove the chicken from the pot and transfer it to a baking dish, meat-side up. Spoon or brush 1 tablespoon of the sauce from the pot over each chicken half. Place the chicken in the oven and bake for 20 minutes, then increase the oven temperature to 200°C fan/220°C/410°F/gas mark 7 and cook for an additional 10 minutes, or until the skin is golden brown and crispy.

Drain the rice and add it to the pot with the sauce. Stir gently to combine, then add 500 ml/2 cups of hot water and the remaining stock cube. Increase the heat to medium–high and bring it to a boil. Once boiling, reduce the heat to low. Cover the pot with a clean kitchen towel and lid, and leave to cook for 20 minutes.

Once done, turn off the heat, remove the towel and replace the lid to allow the rice to rest for a few minutes.

In a frying pan (skillet), heat the remaining 2 tablespoons of ghee or oil over medium heat. Add the flaked almonds and cook until golden brown. Stir in the raisins or sultanas, cooking briefly until they plump up. Remove from the heat.

To serve, spoon the rice onto a large serving dish, creating a bed. Place the roasted chicken in the centre, then drizzle over the almonds and raisins with their oil.

About the author

Ilhan Mohamed Abdi lives in London with her young family and is of Somali heritage. After leaving her corporate job she started cooking meals that had all the flavour and heritage of the dishes she'd grown up enjoying, adapted for a modern cook who may not have time for the traditional marinades and fermentation processes. Instead, Ilhan's recipes use more easily accessible ingredients and simplified methods, without sacrificing on flavour. This is her first book.

Index

A
addas soup 58
adriyad 191
almonds
    Saudi spiced rice with chicken 212
    umm ali (croissant bread pudding) 25
ambaabur 203
apples: broccoli slaw 41
aubergines
    mesa'a'ah (aubergine and tomato stew) 111
    roasted vegetable lasagne 102
avocado smoothie 178

B
baasto isku karis 94
bajiye 42
baklava custard tart 195
bariis Somali 72
barley
    sareen (barley porridge) 31
    shurba (lamb, oat and barley soup) 54
basbousa 155
beans
    fasooliyad (spiced beans) 28
    fuul mudammas (stewed fava beans with eggs and feta) 63
beef
    beef sambuus (samosas) 48–9
    bisteeki (thinly sliced spiced steak) 79
    breaded bisteeki with tomato salad 80–1
    cheeseburger sliders 105
    cheesesteak sandwiches 103
    hummus with spiced beef 57
    macaroni béchamel 76
    nafaqo (Scotch eggs) 53
    sausage rolls 61
    suqaar (diced beef and vegetable sauté) 84

beignets, cardamom-spiced 132
bisbaas cagaar 141
bisbaas qumbe 139
biscuit pudding 151
biscuits: kac kac (fried biscuits) 190
bisteeki 79
Branston pickle: sausage rolls 61
breads 114–15
    bur (cardamom-spiced beignets) 132
    dinner rolls 131
    khaliat nahal (honeycomb bread) 196–9
    kimis (flaky flatbread) 123
    laxoox (fermented pancakes) 117–18
    laxoox with sweetened eggs 33
    muufo (flatbread) 119
    za'atar focaccia 186–7
broccoli slaw 41
bur 132
bur kuus kuus 38–40
buttermilk: fried chicken 88

C
cabbage: maraq (lamb and vegetable broth) 47
cadriyad 191
cakes
    basbousa (semolina cake) 155
    doolsho Somali and cardamom custard 209
    Somali chai tres leches 149
    timir cake (spiced date cake with caramel sauce) 152
cambaabur (spiced and sweetened fermented pancakes) 203
'camel' milk 181
canjeero 33, 117–18
cardamom crème caramel 162
cardamom-spiced beignets 132
carrots
    addas soup (lentil soup) 58

grilled sea bass 98
maraq (lamb and vegetable broth) 47
oxtail stew with soor 90–1
roasted vegetable lasagne 102
Saudi spiced rice with chicken 212
suugo sabaayad (lamb stew) 97
upside-down chicken rice 82
cheese
    cheeseburger sliders 105
    cheesesteak sandwiches 103
    egg bites 30
    fuul mudammas (stewed fava beans with eggs and feta) 63
    kunafa (crispy syrup-soaked pastry with cream) 161
    macaroni béchamel 76
    qatayef (cheese-filled, syrup-soaked sweet pancakes) 210–11
    roasted vegetable lasagne 102
    sausage rolls 61
    sheet pan pizza 105
    stuffed sweet cheese samosas 154
    Yemeni lahsa (stewed spiced tomatoes with eggs and soft cheese) 22
chicken
    as alternative ingredient 54
    chicken swarwarma 108–9
    coconut chicken curry 101
    fried chicken 88
    mini chicken patties 64
    Saudi spiced rice with chicken 212
    upside-down chicken rice 82
chickpeas
    falafel 83
    hummus with spiced beef 57
chillies
    bisbaas cagaar (Somali chilli sauce) 141
    bisbaas qumbe (coconut chilli

sauce) 139
shidni (sweet and spicy chutney) 138
chutney, sweet and spicy 138
cinnamon rolls, mini date 156–7
coconut chicken curry 101
coconut cream: coconut chicken curry 101
coconut, desiccated
   baasto isku karis (one-pot lamb pasta) 94
   basbousa (semolina cake) 155
   bisbaas qumbe (coconut chilli sauce) 139
   umm ali (croissant bread pudding) 25
coconut milk
   addas soup (lentil soup) 58
   oxtail stew with soor 90–1
cod: pan-fried cod 87
coffee
   spiced coffee 171
   tiramisu 150
condensed milk
   avocado smoothie 178
   biscuit pudding 151
   Somali chai tres leches 149
   umm ali (croissant bread pudding) 25
corn ribs 60
courgettes: roasted vegetable lasagne 102
cream
   baklava custard tart 195
   biscuit pudding 151
   doolsho Somali and cardamom custard 209
   Somali chai tres leches 149
   timir cake (spiced date cake with caramel sauce) 152
   tiramisu 150
   umm ali (croissant bread pudding) 25
cream cheese
   khaliat nahal (honeycomb bread) 196–9
   mini date cinnamon rolls 156–7
crème caramel, cardamom 162
croissant bread pudding 25

D

dates
   bisbaas cagaar (Somali chilli sauce) 141
   date shake 21
   mini date cinnamon rolls 156–7
   shidni (sweet and spicy chutney) 138
   timir cake (spiced date cake with caramel sauce) 152
desserts
   baklava custard tart 195
   biscuit pudding 151
   cardamom crème caramel 162
   doolsho Somali and cardamom custard 209
   kunafa (crispy syrup-soaked pastry with cream) 161
   qatayef (cheese-filled, syrup-soaked sweet pancakes) 210–11
   Somali chai tres leches 149
   tiramisu 150
   umm ali (croissant bread pudding) 25
dinner rolls 131
doolsho Somali and cardamom custard 209
drinks
   avocado smoothie 178
   'camel' milk 181
   date shake 21
   mango lassi 177
   mint lemonade 173
   mint tea 172
   qaxwa Somali (spiced coffee) 171
   shaah (spiced tea) 168
   watermelon mocktail 174

E

eggs
   baklava custard tart 195
   cardamom crème caramel 162
   doolsho Somali and cardamom custard 209
   egg bites 30
   fuul mudammas (stewed fava beans with eggs and feta) 63
   laxoox with sweetened eggs 33
   nafaqo (Scotch eggs) 53
   rolex (rolled omelette with flatbread) 24
   Yemeni lahsa (stewed spiced tomatoes with eggs and soft cheese) 22
Eid 184–5
evaporated milk
   khaliat nahal (honeycomb bread) 196–9
   shaah (spiced tea) 168
   Somali chai tres leches 149

F

falafel 83
fasooliyad 28
fish
   grilled sea bass 98
   pan-fried cod 87
   tuna sambuus (samosas) 48–9
focaccia, za'atar 186–7
fuul mudammas 63

G

gherkins: cheeseburger sliders 105

H

hawaash 142
honeycomb bread 196–9
hummus with spiced beef 57

I

iftar 36–7, 70

K

kac kac 190
khaliat nahal 196–9
kimis 123
kunafa (crispy syrup-soaked pastry with cream) 161

L

lamb
- baasto isku karis (one-pot lamb pasta) 94
- lamb chops 75
- maraq (lamb and vegetable broth) 47
- roasted lamb shoulder 204
- shurba (lamb, oat and barley soup) 54
- surbiyan (one-pot lamb rice) 192–3
- suugo sabaayad (lamb stew) 97

laxoox 117–18
- with sweetened eggs 33

lemon-lime soda: 'camel' milk 181

lemons
- baasto isku karis (one-pot lamb pasta) 94
- bisbaas cagaar (Somali chilli sauce) 141
- bisbaas qumbe (coconut chilli sauce) 139
- broccoli slaw 41
- chicken swarwarma 108–9
- grilled sea bass 98
- hummus with spiced beef 57
- mesa'a'ah (aubergine and tomato stew) 111
- mint lemonade 173
- pan-fried cod 87
- potato salad 67

lentils
- addas soup (lentil soup) 58
- bajiye (split pea fritters) 42

limes
- surbiyan (one-pot lamb rice) 192–3
- watermelon mocktail 174

M

macaroni béchamel 76
malawax (malawah) 120
mango lassi 177
maraq 47
mascarpone: tiramisu 150
mayonnaise
- bisbaas qumbe (coconut chilli sauce) 139
- broccoli slaw 41

mesa'a'ah 111

milk
- avocado smoothie 178
- baklava custard tart 195
- bisteeki (thinly sliced spiced steak) 79
- breaded bisteeki with tomato salad 80–1
- bur (cardamom-spiced beignets) 132
- bur kuu kuus (syrup-soaked fried dough balls) 38–40
- cardamom crème caramel 162
- date shake 21
- dinner rolls 131
- doolsho Somali and cardamom custard 209
- khaliat nahal (honeycomb bread) 196–9
- macaroni béchamel 76
- malawax (malawah) 120
- mango lassi 177
- mini date cinnamon rolls 156–7
- roasted vegetable lasagne 102
- shaah (spiced tea) 168
- Somali chai tres leches 149
- umm ali (croissant bread pudding) 25

mint
- mint lemonade 173
- mint tea 172
- watermelon mocktail 174

mushrooms: egg bites 30
muufo 119

N

nac nac loos 200
nafaqo 53

O

oats: shurba (lamb, oat and barley soup) 54
onions
- addas soup (lentil soup) 58
- baasto isku karis (one-pot lamb pasta) 94
- bajiye (split pea fritters) 42
- bariis Somali (aromatic Somali rice) 72
- beef sambuus (samosas) 48–9
- bisteeki (thinly sliced spiced steak) 79
- breaded bisteeki with tomato salad 80–1
- broccoli slaw 41
- cambaabur (spiced and sweetened fermented pancakes) 203
- coconut chicken curry 101
- egg bites 30
- falafel 83
- fasooliyad (spiced beans) 28
- fuul mudammas (stewed fava beans with eggs and feta) 63
- grilled sea bass 98
- macaroni béchamel 76
- mesa'a'ah (aubergine and tomato stew) 111
- mini chicken patties 64
- oxtail stew with soor 90–1
- roasted lamb shoulder 204
- roasted vegetable lasagne 102
- rolex (rolled omelette with flatbread) 24
- shidni (sweet and spicy chutney) 138
- shurba (lamb, oat and barley soup) 54
- suqaar (diced beef and vegetable sauté) 84
- surbiyan (one-pot lamb rice) 192–3
- tuna sambuus (samosas) 48–9
- upside-down chicken rice 82
- Yemeni lahsa (stewed spiced tomatoes with eggs and soft cheese) 22

oxtail stew with soor 90–1

P

pancakes
  cambaabur (spiced and sweetened fermented pancakes) 203
  laxoox (fermented pancakes) 119
  laxoox with sweetened eggs 33
  malawax (malawah) 120
passata: roasted vegetable lasagne 102
pasta
  baasto isku karis (one-pot lamb pasta) 94
  catriyat (sweetened vermicelli) 191
  macaroni béchamel 76
  roasted vegetable lasagne 102
peanut brittle 200
pepperoni: sheet pan pizza 105
peppers
  bisteeki (thinly sliced spiced steak) 79
  cheesesteak sandwiches 103
  egg bites 30
  fasooliyad (spiced beans) 28
  grilled sea bass 98
  roasted vegetable lasagne 102
  suqaar (diced beef and vegetable sauté) 84
  suugo sabaayad (lamb stew) 97
  tuna sambuus (samosas) 48-9
  upside-down chicken rice 82
pesto: macaroni béchamel 76
pickles
  cheeseburger sliders 105
  chicken swarwarma 108-9
pine nuts: hummus with spiced beef 57
pistachios
  baklava custard tart 195
  kunafa (crispy syrup-soaked pastry with cream) 161
  qatayef (cheese-filled, syrup-soaked sweet pancakes) 210-11
  Somali chai tres leches 149
  stuffed sweet cheese samosas 154
  umm ali (croissant bread pudding) 25

pizza, sheet pan 105
planning for meals 12-14
porridge, barley 31
potatoes
  falafel 83
  maraq (lamb and vegetable broth) 47
  potato salad 67
  suugo sabaayad (lamb stew) 97
  upside-down chicken rice 82

Q

qatayef 210-11
qaxwa Somali (spiced coffee) 171
quail eggs: nafaqo (Scotch eggs) 53

R

raisins
  broccoli slaw 41
  catriyat (sweetened vermicelli) 191
  Saudi spiced rice with chicken 212
Ramadan 6-7, 9
ras el hanout: addas soup (lentil soup) 58
rice
  bariis Somali (aromatic Somali rice) 72
  sareen (barley porridge) 31
  Saudi spiced rice with chicken 212
  surbiyan (one-pot lamb rice) 192-3
  upside-down chicken rice 82
rolex 24

S

sabaayad 123
sambuus (samosas)
  filled 48-9
  sheets 126
  stuffed sweet cheese samosas 154
sareen 31
sauces
  bisbaas cagaar (Somali chilli sauce) 141

bisbaas qumbe (coconut chilli sauce) 139
Saudi kabsa 212
sausage rolls 61
sea bass: grilled sea bass 98
semolina
  basbousa (semolina cake) 155
  oxtail stew with soor 90-1
shaah (spiced tea) 168
shallots: bisbaas qumbe (coconut chilli sauce) 139
shidni 138
shurbad 54
Somali chai tres leches 149
Somali chilli sauce 141
Somali lentil fritters 42
Somali spice mix 142
Somalia 8
sorghum flour
  cambaabur (spiced and sweetened fermented pancakes) 203
  laxoox (fermented pancakes) 117-18
soups
  addas soup (lentil soup) 58
  maraq (lamb and vegetable broth) 47
  shurba (lamb, oat and barley soup) 54
spinach: egg bites 30
split peas: bajiye (split pea fritters) 42
spring onions: oxtail stew with soor 90-1
stewed fava beans with eggs and feta 63
suhoor 18-19
sultanas
  bariis Somali (aromatic Somali rice) 72
  Saudi spiced rice with chicken 212
  surbiyan (one-pot lamb rice) 192-3
suqaar 84
surbiyan 192-3
suugo sabaayad 97

T

tahini: hummus with spiced beef 57
tamarind
    bisbaas cagaar (Somali chilli sauce) 141
    shidni (sweet and spicy chutney) 138
    suqaar (diced beef and vegetable sauté) 84
    surbiyan (one-pot lamb rice) 192–3
tarts: baklava custard tart 195
tea
    mint 172
    spiced 168
timir cake 152
tiramisu 150
tomatoes
    baasto isku karis (one-pot lamb pasta) 94
    bariis Somali (aromatic Somali rice) 72
    bisbaas cagaar (Somali chilli sauce) 141
    bisteeki (thinly sliced spiced steak) 79
    breaded bisteeki with tomato salad 80–1
    coconut chicken curry 101
    fuul mudammas (stewed fava beans with eggs and feta) 63
    macaroni béchamel 76
    maraq (lamb and vegetable broth) 47
    mesa'a'ah (aubergine and tomato stew) 111
    mini chicken patties 64
    roasted lamb shoulder 204
    roasted vegetable lasagne 102
    rolex (rolled omelette with flatbread) 24
    sheet pan pizza 105
    shidni (sweet and spicy chutney) 138
    shurba (lamb, oat and barley soup) 54
    suqaar (diced beef and vegetable sauté) 84
    surbiyan (one-pot lamb rice) 192–3
    suugo sabaayad (lamb stew) 97
    Yemeni lahsa (stewed spiced tomatoes with eggs and soft cheese) 22
tuna: tuna sambuus (samosas) 48–9

U

umm ali 25

V

vermicelli, sweetened 191

W

watermelon mocktail 174

X

xawaash 142

Y

Yemeni lahsa 22
yogurt
    avocado smoothie 178
    basbousa (semolina cake) 155
    bisbaas qumbe (coconut chilli sauce) 139
    broccoli slaw 41
    'camel' milk 181
    mango lassi 177
    muufo (flatbread) 119
    roasted lamb shoulder 204
    sareen (barley porridge) 31
    surbiyan (one-pot lamb rice) 192–3

Z

za'atar focaccia 186–7

Acknowledgements

All praise belongs to the Almighty. Without His guidance and mercy, none of this would be possible. I want to especially acknowledge those observing Ramadan while carrying quiet struggles. May your efforts be accepted, and your burdens lightened. You are a reminder of what resilience and devotion look like.

To my *Hooyo Macaan* (sweet mother), thank you for instilling in me a love for this month, and for the food and rituals that make it feel so special. You gave meaning to every meal, and I carry that with me in every dish I make. This love of cooking came from yours. Thank you for helping me test nearly every recipe in this book, for staying up late when you didn't have to, and for being there in every way that matters.

To my siblings, thank you for always being there. For your encouragement, for your honesty, and especially for keeping me calm when everything felt overwhelming. You have no idea how much that means to me.

To my nieces and nephews, your support, your excitement, your belief in me has meant more than you know. You cheer me on like I'm someone extraordinary, and that kind of love is a gift I don't take for granted. Thank you for always making me feel seen.

To my closest friends – you know who you are. Thank you for being there through every stage of this process, for testing recipes without complaint, for your honest feedback, and for always showing up with love and encouragement. Whether it was a voice note, a taste test, or just reminding me to keep going, you were part of this book in more ways than you know.

To my mother-in-law, your generosity and warmth never go unnoticed. Thank you for sharing your knowledge, your recipes, and for being there when I need you most, like sending *kimis* at 6am when I was too exhausted to move. I'm endlessly grateful.

To Lucy, my editor, thank you for setting this book in motion. Thank you for believing in me from the start and guiding it with such care. Thank you for allowing me to execute my vision without restriction and for helping shape these pages into something I'm proud of. To Lily and Laura, thank you for all your help with the design and the beautiful details throughout. Thank you for your support and encouragement, and bringing to life what feels true to me.

To Liz and Max, thank you for capturing these recipes in ways I couldn't have imagined. You brought this book to life visually, with a sensitivity and beauty that honoured every bite and every story. And thank you to Flossy for styling the food so beautifully, and to Susannah for bringing these recipes to life so patiently, even with all my questions and constant hovering.

To my community, those who follow, comment, cook along, and share. I wouldn't be writing this without you. You've turned simple recipes into something much more: connection, comfort and celebration. Thank you for being part of this journey.

To my daughter, you are the heart behind this book. Even though you're still too young to fully understand it, everything in these pages was written with you in mind. This is something I want you to have, to hold, and one day to pass down to your own children, God willing. A piece of who I am, and where we come from. You are the reason I want to preserve these memories and these meals.

And to my husband, Shermarke. You are my quiet anchor and the reason I get to do this. Your encouragement is steady, your support unwavering, and your belief in me never fades, not even when mine does. Thank you for holding everything up behind the scenes and making space for this dream.

Pavilion
An imprint of HarperCollins*Publishers* Ltd
1 London Bridge Street
London SE1 9GF

www.harpercollins.co.uk

HarperCollins*Publishers*
Macken House
39/40 Mayor Street Upper,
Dublin 1
D01 C9W8
Ireland

10 9 8 7 6 5 4 3 2

First published in Great Britain by Pavilion
An imprint of HarperCollins*Publishers* 2026

Copyright © Pavilion 2026
Text © Ilhan Mohamed Abdi 2026

Ilhan Mohamed Abdi asserts the moral right to be identified as the author of this work. A catalogue record of this book is available from the British Library.

ISBN 978-0-00-874306-2

Publishing Director: Laura Russell
Commissioning Editor: Lucy Smith
Editor: Kate Reeves-Brown
Editorial Assistant: Daisy Gudmunsen
Proofreader: Rebecca Woods
Indexer: Ruth Ellis
Designer: Lily Wilson
Production Controller: Grace O'Byrne
Photographer: Haarala Hamilton
Food Stylist: Flossy McAslan
Food Stylist Assistant: Susannah Cohen
Prop Stylist: Charlie Phillips
Prop Stylist Assistant: Olivia Axson
Layout designer: James Boast

Printed and bound by GPS Group in Bosnia and Herzegovina

All rights reserved. No part of this publication may be reproduced, stored in a retrieval system, or transmitted, in any form or by any means, electronic, mechanical, photocopying, recording or otherwise, without the prior written permission of the publishers.

Without limiting the author's and publisher's exclusive rights, any unauthorised use of this publication to train generative artificial intelligence (AI) technologies is expressly prohibited. HarperCollins also exercise their rights under Article 4(3) of the Digital Single Market Directive 2019/790 and expressly reserve this publication from the text and data mining exception.

WHEN USING KITCHEN APPLIANCES PLEASE ALWAYS FOLLOW THE MANUFACTURER'S INSTRUCTIONS.